D0235728

CAN'T FAIL CAKES

MITZIE WILSON'S

CAN'T FAIL CAKES

To my new daughter, Angelica Lois

Published in 1995 by Merehurst Limited
Ferry House, 51-57 Lacy Road, Putney, London SW15 1PR

ISBN 1-85391-431-2

A catalogue record for this book is available from the British Library.

Editor: Beverly Le Blanc
Series Designer: Roger Hammond
Designers: Roger Daniels and Mike Rose
Photographer: Huw Williams
Home economist: Kathy Man
Home economist's assistants: Kate O'Donnell and Katy Holder
Stylist: Suzy Gittins
Typesetter: Nigel Burns

Colour separation by Global Colour, Malaysia
Printed in Singapore by CS Graphics Pte Ltd

NOTES

A standard spoon measurement is used in all recipes:

1 teaspoon = one 5 ml spoon
1 tablespoon = one 15 ml spoon
All spoon measures are rounded.

All eggs are size 3 unless otherwise specified.

Ovens should be preheated to the specified temperature.

For all recipes, quantities are given metric and imperial. Follow one set of measures but not a mixture as they are not interchangeable.

Frontispiece: Wensleydale Apple Cake, *see page 56*

FOREWORD

This cake book has been a pleasure to write. I have been collecting cake recipes for years and at last they are all written down in one tome, with every recipe tested at least twice, if not three times, too!

I love making cakes. Whenever I'm bored I find myself wanting to bake. It is very therapeutic and satisfying, even if these days I end up freezing half the cake to eat later... more a case of out of temptation's way, rather than lack of greed! I am always experimenting with new recipes, but as life is so busy I try to make quick all-in-one cakes or ones without too many fancy fillings and icings.

I've had fun experimenting while writing this book, and you'll find some real winners developed with a lot of trial and effort. There is a definite formula for making cakes and you can't mess about with the fat, flour and sugar ratio, so every time I tried to cut down on the cholesterol or the sweetness, the cake suffered as a result. The trial cakes may have been healthier, but they were usually stodgier and never good enough to be included in this book. My husband, Dave, was the perfect tester, he would say "this is so healthy it will stay in the tin and go mouldy"... and it was always the case.

I really do believe that cakes are to be enjoyed. Because we don't eat them every day, if you want a slice of cake it has to be really delicious. (I have eaten one or two slices of cake every day for six months and I've put on a stone in weight... that's because I'm six months pregnant. I'm just hoping my baby won't have an incredibly sweet tooth!)

The title *Can't Fail Cakes* has made me completely neurotic. Anyone can bake a cake that doesn't turn out properly, but I promise you that every recipe has been double, if not triple, tested by friends who aren't home economists or professional bakers. They are keen amateurs, like I hope most of you who use this book will be. I think this was important because I can take so much for granted. Thanks go in particular to Lydia Sidaway and Nichola Tester, who's critical comments have been very valuable.

I do hope you will take the time to read the introduction and that you enjoy making the cakes and eating them. Before you weigh any ingredients, please read the Secrets of Successful Baking on page 9.

Happy Baking!

Mitzie

Introduction

Chocolate cakes

Fresh cakes

Dried fruit cakes

page 62

Traditional cakes

page 78

Loaf cakes

page 86

INTRODUCTION

You'll find most of the cakes in this book are good family cakes that keep well in a tin for at least a week, are ideal for packed lunches and for feeding hungry kids when they come home from school. There are, of course, the more elaborate gâteaux, too, as I can never miss the opportunity to make a cake for an alfresco Sunday lunch, for a special picnic at an outdoor music concert, for someone's birthday surprise, or for a dinner or supper party. Also, this book would not be complete without my mother's wedding cake recipe, which both she and I have been making for years. But if you're looking for something less traditional, there's also a white chocolate wedding cake recipe, as this style of celebration cake is becoming more and more popular.

Many of my recipes have been collected over the years from magazines, such as *Woman's Own*, *Family Circle* and *Best*, where I worked before becoming editor of *BBC Good Food*. As editor I have far less time in the kitchen, but I always make sure I'm there when the cakes are being tested to give my taste approval. Some of my favourites from *BBC Good Food* are included in this book.

This book was planned to make it as useful and comprehensive as possible, so I've included lots of traditional favourites, such as Dundee Cake, Swiss Roll and Victoria Sandwich, and there are lots of variations on fruit cakes which you can make for Christmas.

After trying what seems like hundreds of chocolate cakes, I've whittled my selection down to the very best, including everything from a classic rich Austrian Sachertorte to White Chocolate Flake Gâteau for a right up-to-the-minute recipe that can turn any occasion into something special. I haven't, however, included recipes for yeast cakes, pastries or biscuits.

However, I hope there is a balance of healthy cakes for you. Whenever possible I have included wholemeal flour as it does give a lovely nutty flavour, I've chosen fresh seasonal fruits to sweeten cakes rather than icing in many recipes, and I've used sunflower margarine or oil, rather than butter, to make the lighter all-in-one cakes. This is partly to help save on cholesterol, but also to make them very quick to prepare. I do, however, use a lot of butter in the traditional cakes as I believe the flavour is so much better than margarine. You can use block margarine instead if you want to make huge savings at the supermarket.

I also love to include the excellent range of dried fruits available in my recipes, not relying on just sultanas and raisins. You'll find lots of recipes that make the most of dried apricots, dates, figs and mango and crystallised ginger, as well as lots of nuts, too.

All the recipes were tested in conventional ovens. I did not test them in a fan-assisted oven as manufacturers' temperatures vary, so sadly you will have to adjust the timings according to the instructions in your manual if this is the type of oven you have. But I know from the hundreds of letters I have received over the years working in the cookery departments of so many magazines, that one major cause of disappointment are cakes baked in fan-assisted ovens. Follow my recipes and look up your oven handbook.

SECRETS OF SUCCESSFUL BAKING

- All eggs are size 3 unless otherwise stated. Lightly beat the eggs before adding them to other ingredients.

- Use sunflower margarine or soft-tub margarine that is full fat and has a label that states it can be used for baking. Low-fat margarines contain too much water to be used in cake mixtures.

- I recommend you have butter or margarine at room temperature before you cream it with sugar. Not only will it be easier to beat, but you will also get a lighter cake.

- All my spoon measurements are rounded, not heaped.

- If you sift the flour, you will get a lighter textured crumb.

- To measure golden syrup, treacle or honey accurately, dip the spoon in boiling water or warm it over a flame before measuring. This way the syrup, treacle or honey falls off it easily without any being left on the spoon.

- Ensure that muscovado sugar is broken up before you add it to other ingredients, otherwise it can be difficult to disperse. I often recommend unrefined sugars for the best flavour.

- Always use the tin size specified in the recipe. Usually, however, you can use a square tin 2.5 cm (1 in) smaller than a round tin.

- Never forget to preheat the oven to the specified temperature so it will be hot enough when the cake mixture is ready to be baked.

- For fan-assisted ovens adjust the temperature according to manufacturers' instructions. The temperature should often be set lower than the setting in a conventional oven. Baking time may also be faster. I think the texture of cakes baked in fan-assisted ovens is sometimes drier and more crumbly than those baked in conventional ovens.

- You can tell when a cake is baked when it feels just firm to the touch in the centre and if you press it lightly it springs back and not feel as if you have crushed it or leave a dent. A properly baked cake should not wobble in the centre, it will have begun to shrink from the sides of the tin and if you pierce the centre of the cake with a skewer it should come out clean. If the skewer comes out sticky, return the cake to the oven to bake a little longer.

- If a cake begins to over-brown before it is baked, place a double layer of greaseproof paper on top.

TYPES OF CAKES

CREAMED CAKES

The classic creamed cake is, of course, The Victoria Sandwich. Creamed cakes have a lovely, soft, rich crumb with a delicious flavour of butter (although you can use margarine).

For success, be sure you remove the butter or margarine from the fridge at least 30 minutes before making cakes to bring it to room temperature, or warm it slightly first. This makes it easier to cream with the sugar, so you should get a lighter result. To cream the butter or margarine and sugar, put them into a bowl and beat with a wooden spoon or electric whisk until the mixture becomes very pale in colour and is very creamy or fluffy in texture. The more you beat it at this stage, the more air you will incorporate into the mixture and the lighter the cake will be.

Also make sure the eggs are at room temperature because if they are cold they can make the fat coagulate and curdle. Add the eggs very gradually, beating between additions to give an emulsion. If the mixture does curdle, add a spoonful of the measured flour.

Sift the flour before folding it into the cake mixture, then use a large metal spoon to fold it in. I use a slotted draining spoon.

To fold in the flour, spoon the mixture from the bottom of the bowl and fold it up over the top. Do this in a figure-of-eight movement, cutting through the mixture to make sure there are no pockets of flour.

ALL-IN-ONE CAKES

All-in-one cakes tend to have a crumbly, fine texture depending on how well the mixture is beaten. Baking powder is used as a raising agent. These are so simple to make, but you must ensure that you buy the correct soft-tub margarine or the texture of the cake will be wrong and the mixture may separate and the fruit may sink. It must be high-fat (low-fat margarines contain too much water) and it is advisable to check that the label states that the margarine can be used for baking. I like sunflower margarine for its flavour. If you want to use oil instead, choose a bland flavour such as sunflower or rapeseed oil.

To make this style of cake, all the ingredients are simply beaten together in a bowl at once, but take care not to over-mix it or the cake may be tough. If you use a wooden spoon, just beat for 1 to 2 minutes.

WHISKED CAKES

These cakes are very light in texture and used mostly for gâteaux and dessert cakes.

Whisk the eggs and sugar until they hold a definite trail when the whisk is lifted. You should be able to write the letter 'M' on top and count to 6 before it sinks back into the mixture. Either use an electric hand-held whisk and whisk the eggs and sugar together in a large heatproof bowl over (but not touching) a saucepan of gently simmering (not boiling) water, or whisk them together in the bowl of an electric table-top mixer. It will take about 10 minutes.

Having whisked in all the air it is then vital that you don't knock it all out when you add the flour, so gently fold in the sifted flour with a large metal spoon; gently spoon the mixture from the bottom of the bowl up over the top in a figure-of-eight pattern.

ABOUT CAKE TINS AND HOW TO LINE THEM

I have used a basic range of cake tins that are readily available. If you go shopping for tins, however, you will soon discover the measurements vary; some manufacturers measure from the outside edge, while others measure from the inside edge, but this should not make a great deal of difference to the result. I measure my tins from the inside edge. In this book most of the recipes specify deep or springform cake tins, although some use shallower sandwich tins, loaf tins and Swiss roll tins.

LINING CAKE TINS

Some bakers say you should line the base and sides of cake tins, but I only line the base of shallow sandwich and deep cake tins for most recipes. But for richer cakes which require long, slow baking, such as fruit cakes, you should use a double layer of greaseproof paper. I usually use the paper wrappers from butter or margarine, or a product called everlasting plastic-coated baking sheet. Several brands of this are available and once you cut out the lining to fit your tins, it should last for many months.

LINING THE SIDES OF ROUND TINS

To line the sides of a deep round cake tin or a springform tin, measure the circumference around the cake tin and cut one or two strips the correct length and 2.5 cm (1 in) higher than the tin. Fold up 2.5 cm (1 in) along one long edge. Make slanting cuts every 2.5 cm (1 in) along this edge up to the fold. Grease the tin with melted butter or margarine or vegetable oil and press the strip against the inside with the slashed edges in the base. This will help the paper lie flat, which can be difficult to get correct in a round tin.

LINING THE SIDES OF SQUARE TINS

To line the sides of a deep square tin, cut out strips of greaseproof paper that are slightly longer than each side, but 2.5 cm (1 in) higher. Cut and fold the strips as above, then put them in position, overlapping and folding smoothly in the corners.

LINING BASES

To line the base of a round or square cake tin, place the base on the paper and draw around the outside edge. Cut out the circle or square, then place it in the base.

LINING SWISS ROLL TINS

Cut a sheet of greaseproof paper about 4 cm (1½ in) larger than the tin all the way around. Place the tin on the paper and mark the corners, then cut diagonally into the corners. Grease the tin with melted butter or margarine or vegetable oil and place the paper inside, overlapping the corner cuts. Grease the paper if the recipe specifies.

LINING LOAF TINS

Line it the same way as for a Swiss roll tin but cut the paper at least 15 cm (6 in) larger than the top of the tin. In fact, I usually just put the wrappers from packs of butter over the base and up the two wide sides. A cake baked this way won't win any awards at a WI competition but it still tastes just as good – and saves time!

WHAT WENT WRONG?

UNDER-BAKED

It is likely the oven was not preheated to the specified temperature before the cake was placed in the oven. Putting the raw mixture in the oven instantly reduces the temperature and it then takes longer to come back up to the correct temperature, so the timing should have been increased. The cake's texture will be altered. Baking at the correct temperature is particularly important with large rich fruit cakes, as they are so dense and can take a lot longer to bake if the oven is not preheated correctly.

I have had numerous letters from upset readers over the years who say that their Christmas cake was still not baked after 5 or 6 hours, and I am certain this is the reason. Also ovens do vary and can be as much as 10 to 20 degrees less than the temperature gauge indicates. When cooking at a low temperature, this is critical. If in doubt, I suggest you buy an oven thermometer.

Also, did you use the size cake tin specified in the recipe? If a smaller tin than the one specified is used, the mixture will be deeper and require longer baking.

OVER-BAKED

The reverse applies here. Was the oven temperature set correctly? Or, is your oven possibly 10 or 20 degrees hotter than the temperature gauge indicates? If the cake was baked in a fan-assisted oven did you remember to adjust the temperature and timing according to the manufacturer's instructions? Was the cake tin too large so that the mixture spread out too thinly?

Remember that if the top of the cake appears to be browning too quickly, cover it with a double thickness of greaseproof paper.

SUNKEN MIDDLE

This is usually indicates that the mixture was under-baked. Was your oven at the correct temperature when the cake went in? Did you use a cake tin that was smaller than the one specified in the recipe? This causes the mixture to be too thick to bake in the specified time.

Once the cake is baked and cooled there is little you can do to remedy this problem, except cut a circle out of the middle and serve the cake as a ring cake.

CRUSTY TOP

This is often caused by too much sugar in the mixture, so reduce the sugar slightly the next time you make the cake. Did you measure the golden syrup or treacle accurately? To do this is to warm the spoon in hot water or over a flame before you measure the syrup.

OILY TEXTURE

Did you use the correct margarine? Before you start making a cake mixture, make sure the margarine you are using is a high-fat soft margarine with a label that specifies it can be used for baking. I find that when students come into magazine kitchens to test recipes, one of their common mistakes is to use a low-fat margarine that contains too much water. As a result, the little fat it does contain tends to separate out, making the cake's texture too oily to be nice.

It is also possible you have over-beaten the mixture. This is particularly true when making all-in-one cakes. Unfortunately, it is difficult to tell you exactly when to stop beating and it is something you will just have to learn from experience. The mixture should be smooth and shiny but don't worry about getting every little lump out.

Was the oven temperature too low when the cake went in?

FRUIT SANK

This can be caused by a variety of reasons, including the oven not being preheated to the correct temperature. If it is too low, the mixture does not set quickly enough to support the fruit while the mixture bakes. Also, over-beating the mixture or having it curdle may result in the fruit sinking. If the mixture looks like it is beginning to curdle, stir in a little of the measured flour.

DRY TEXTURE, ESPECIALLY ON EDGES OR THE CRUST

This often indicates that the cake was over-baked. Double check that the oven was preheated to the correct temperature. Did you adjust a fan-assisted oven's temperature and the timing according to the manufacturer's instructions? Did you use the size eggs specified in the recipe?

When you make creamed cakes, the mixture should have a soft dropping consistency so it falls easily away from the spoon when you are ready to spread it in the prepared pan. If it doesn't, beat in 1 to 2 tablespoons milk.

A FLAT CAKE THAT DIDN'T RISE PROPERLY

In a whisked cake, the eggs and sugar were probably not whisked until the mixture left a definite trail when the whisks were lifted. You should be able to count to six before the trail sinks back into the mixture. Another possibility is that the flour was not gently folded in with a large metal spoon.

In other cakes, look at your containers of baking powder or self-raising flour and make sure they are not past the use-by date. Also, double check to make sure you did not leave out the baking powder by mistake.

Did you cream the mixture until very light and fluffy and fold in the flour carefully? Was the oven preheated to the correct temperature?

CAKE CRACKED AND NOT BAKED THROUGH

This can be caused by the oven being too hot when the mixture was put in to bake so that the top baked quickly and the mixture underneath had to force its way up as it baked and rose.

Chocolate cakes

I cooked and eliminated many chocolate cakes before I came to this ultimate selection. I hope you'll agree with me that each one is a winner. Simple or elegant, whatever the occasion or whoever you are making it for, I'm sure there's a cake in this chapter to suit.

DEVIL'S FOOD CAKE

Time to make: 50 minutes
Time to bake: 35 to 45 minutes
Makes a 20 cm (8 in) round cake that cuts into 10 slices

375 ml (12 fl oz) milk
4 teaspoons lemon juice
185 g (6 oz) unsalted butter, at room temperature
410 g (13 oz) caster sugar
3 eggs, size 3
375 g (12 oz) plain flour
1½ teaspoons bicarbonate of soda
90 g (3 oz) cocoa powder
chocolate curls, see page 36, to decorate

Filling

155 ml (5 fl oz) whipping cream
155 ml (5 fl oz) soured cream

American Frosting

375 g (12 oz) caster sugar
½ teaspoon cream of tartar
2 egg whites, size 3

Storing and Freezing

Store for up to 3 days in a cake tin.

Freeze the un-filled and un-iced cakes for up to 3 months in plastic bags or airtight containers. Defrost for 5 to 6 hours at room temperature, then fill and ice.

Spreading American frosting over a Devil's Food Cake.

This is a fabulous triple-decker American-style cake of dark chocolate with a contrasting white frosting, although I should warn not to even attempt this frosting in hot weather. I know from experience that it simply won't set on a hot day.

1 Measure the milk into a measuring jug and add the lemon juice, then set aside to sour. Set the oven to 180C, 350F, Gas 4. Grease three 20 cm (8 in) straight-sided sandwich tins and line the bases with greaseproof paper.
2 Put the butter and half the sugar into a bowl and cream until light and fluffy, then beat in the remaining sugar and the eggs, adding a little of the flour if the mixture begins to curdle.
3 Sift together the remaining flour, bicarbonate of soda and cocoa powder. Add half the soured milk and sifted flour to the creamed mixture and whisk together well, then whisk in remaining milk and flour.
4 Spread the mixture equally between the prepared tins and level the tops. Bake in the centre of the oven for 35 to 40 minutes until firm to the touch.
5 Allow the cakes to cool for 10 minutes in the tins, then turn them out on to wire racks, peel off the lining papers and leave to cool completely.
6 Meanwhile, to make the filling, put the cream into a bowl and whip until it just holds its shape. Beat in 2 tablespoons of the soured cream, then fold in the remainder. Chill until required.
7 If the cakes have risen unevenly, slice off the top of one for a level finish. Sandwich the cakes together with the cream mixture, with the trimmed cake on top.
8 To make the American frosting, place the sugar, cream of tartar and egg whites into a large heatproof bowl over a pan of simmering water. Using an electric hand-held whisk, whisk continuously until the mixture holds it's shape like glossy meringue. This will take 3 to 4 minutes. You will feel the icing beginning to crystallise on the bottom of the bowl.
9 Spread the icing over the top and sides of the cake, swirling it with a palette knife. Decorate with chocolate curls.

SEVILLE ORANGE MARBLE CAKE

Time to make: 35 minutes, plus letting the crystallised orange rind set
Time to bake: 1¼ to 1½ hours
Makes a 20 cm (8 in) round cake that cuts into 8 slices

1 unwaxed Seville orange
90 g (3 oz) plain chocolate
60 g (2 oz) candied orange peel
250 g (8 oz) butter, softened
250 g (8 oz) caster sugar
4 eggs, size 3, lightly beaten and at room temperature
250 g (8 oz) self-raising flour
2 tablespoons cocoa powder

Decoration

1 unwaxed Seville orange
30 g (1 oz) caster sugar

Dark Cocoa Icing

90 g (3 oz) butter
125 g (4 oz) caster sugar
60 g (2 oz) cocoa powder
185 g (6 oz) icing sugar

Storing and Freezing
Store for up to 1 week in a cake tin.
Open freeze until the icing is firm, then freeze for up to 2 months in a plastic bag or an airtight container. Defrost for 6 to 8 hours at room temperature.

I find the combination of chocolate and orange is always a winner. This dark, rich and intensely fruity cake is perfect for a special occasion, such as a birthday party when you want to serve something out of the ordinary. I first came across this recipe in Whicked Chocolate by Jane Suthering, but have adapted it slightly.

1 Set the oven to 180C, 350F, Gas 4. Grease a 20 cm (8 in) round deep or springform cake tin and line the base with greaseproof paper. Grate the orange rind and set aside, then cut the orange in half and squeeze out 2 tablespoons juice. Set the juice aside. Finely chop the chocolate, then finely chop the peel.
2 Cream the butter and sugar together until light and fluffy. Beat in the eggs, adding a little of the flour if the mixture begins to curdle. Sift over the remaining flour, then fold it in. Divide the mixture equally between 2 mixing bowls.
3 To make the orange mixture, add the peel, orange rind and 2 tablespoons orange juice to one bowl and fold in.
4 To make the chocolate mixture, sift the cocoa powder into the second bowl, then add the chopped chocolate and fold in.
5 Place alternate spoonfuls of the mixtures in the prepared tin, then use a knife to swirl together. Bake for 1¼ to 1½ hours until firm. Cool in the tin for 5 minutes, then turn it out on to a wire rack, peel off the lining paper and leave the cake to cool.
6 Meanwhile, make the decoration. Use a potato peeler to pare the orange rind without any pith, then cut the rind into fine shreds. Bring a small saucepan of water to the boil, then add the orange shreds and boil for 2 to 3 minutes. Drain well, then dry the orange shreds on plenty of kitchen paper. When dry, toss them in the caster sugar, then allow to set for at least 1 hour.
7 To make the dark cocoa icing, place the butter, caster sugar and 4 tablespoons water into a saucepan over a low heat. Stir until the sugar dissolves, then bring to the simmering point for 1 to 2 minutes. Remove from the heat and set aside. Sift cocoa powder and icing sugar together, then add to the pan and beat until smooth. Cool until thick enough to spread.
8 Swirl the icing over the top and sides of the cake, then sprinkle the top with the crystallised orange shreds.

WHITE CHOCOLATE PECAN CAKE

Time to make: 30 minutes
Time to bake: 50 minutes
Makes a 20 cm (8 in) round cake that cuts into 10 slices

60 g (2 oz) pecans
185 g (6 oz) white chocolate
185 g (6 oz) butter, at room temperature
185 g (6 oz) light muscovado sugar
3 eggs, size 3, beaten and at room temperature
185 g (6 oz) self-raising flour
60 g (2 oz) pecans, to decorate

Rippled Toffee Icing
125 g (4 oz) creamy toffees
200 ml (7 fl oz) double cream

Storing and Freezing
Store the un-filled and un-decorated cake for up to 4 days. Once filled, keep it in the fridge and eat within 2 days.

Freeze the un-filled and decorated cake for up to 2 months in a plastic bag or an airtight container. Defrost for 5 to 6 hours at room temperature, then fill and decorate.

A stunning cake to serve for dinner parties. The cake is flavoured with white chocolate and ground pecans and filled with melted toffees and cream.

1 Set the oven to 180C, 350F, Gas 4. Grease a 20 cm (8 in) round deep cake tin and line the base with greaseproof paper. Put the pecans into a food processor and whizz until they are finely ground. Break the chocolate into a heatproof bowl over a pan of simmering water and stir until it melts. (Or, melt in a microwave on High for 2½ minutes.)
2 Put the butter and sugar into a bowl and cream together until light and fluffy. Gradually beat in the eggs, adding a little of the flour if the mixture begins to curdle. Stir in the melted white chocolate. Sift over the remaining flour and use a large metal spoon to fold it in along with the ground pecans and 1 to 2 tablespoons of milk to give a soft dropping consistency.
3 Spread the mixture in the prepared tin and level the top. Bake in the centre of the oven for 50 minutes until golden and firm to the touch. Cool in the tin for 10 minutes, then turn it out on to a wire rack, peel off the lining paper and cool completely.
4 Meanwhile, to make the icing, put the toffees and 3 tablespoons of the cream into a heatproof bowl over a pan of gently simmering water and stir until the toffees melt. (Or, melt in a microwave on High for 1 to 2 minutes.) Lightly whip the cream until it just holds its shape. Stir the toffees gently through the cream to give a rippled effect. Chill until required.
5 Sandwich the cakes together with half of the cream mixture, then spread the remainder on top of the cake. Decorate with the pecans.

CHOCOLATE BRANDY TRUFFLE CAKE

Time to make: 40 minutes, plus chilling
Time to bake: 45 minutes
Makes a 20 cm (8 in) round cake that cuts into 8 to 10 slices

220 g (7 oz) plain chocolate
125 g (4 oz) butter
3 eggs, size 3, separated and at room temperature
125 g (4 oz) light muscovado sugar
60 ml (2 fl oz) brandy
90 g (3 oz) self-raising flour
60 g (2 oz) ground almonds

Chocolate Crème

1 tablespoon cornflour
155 ml (5 fl oz) milk
3 tablespoons caster sugar
2 egg yolks, size 3
90 g (3 oz) plain chocolate
185 g (6 oz) butter, at room temperature
90 g (3 oz) icing sugar

Decorations

cocoa powder, optional
icing sugar, optional
chocolate curls, see page 36, optional

This is one of my favourite chocolate cakes as it is so moist and it rises evenly with a slightly crusty top. The brandy gives it a lovely rich flavour but you can also use rum or Amaretti, or if you prefer not to use any alcohol, substitute milk instead. The icing is also a favourite as it is basically a chocolate custard, enriched with butter and is not too sweet. It spreads well and is easy to make into truffles or pipe.

1 Set the oven to 180C, 350F, Gas 4. Grease a 20 cm (8 in) round deep cake tin and line the base with greaseproof paper.
2 Break the chocolate into a heatproof bowl over a saucepan of simmering water. Dice the butter, then add it to the pan and stir until the chocolate and butter melt and are blended together. (Or, melt in a microwave on High for 2 to 3 minutes.) Remove the bowl from the heat and set aside to cool slightly.
3 Place the egg yolks and sugar into a large bowl. Use an electric hand-held whisk and whisk until the mixture become pale brown and creamy. Stir the brandy into the chocolate mixture, then gradually whisk it into the yolk mixture.
4 Sift the flour and ground almonds over the chocolate mixture, then use a large metal spoon to fold in.
5 Put the egg whites into a clean grease-free bowl and whisk until they form stiff peaks. Use the large metal spoon to fold them into the cake mixture until evenly blended.
6 Spread the mixture in the prepared tin and level the top. Bake in the centre of the oven for 45 minutes or until firm to the touch. Allow the cake to cool in the tin for 10 minutes, then turn it out on to a wire rack, peel off the lining paper and leave to cool completely.
7 Meanwhile, to make the chocolate crème, place the cornflour into a saucepan and stir in the milk, then place the pan over a medium heat. Add the sugar and bring to the boil, stirring constantly. Remove the pan from the heat and beat in the egg yolks. Return the pan to a low heat and cook for 1 minute, stirring constantly, then remove from the heat. Break the

Chocolate Brandy Truffle Cake

Continued on page 20

Chocolate Brandy Truffle Cake *continued from page 18*

Storing and Freezing
Store the cake for up to 5 days in the fridge.

Open freeze until the icing is firm, then wrap in a plastic bag or put in an airtight container. Freeze for up to 1 month. Defrost in a cool place for 6 to 8 hours.

chocolate into the pan and stir until it melts. Set aside to cool.
8 Put the butter into a bowl and beat until smooth, then beat in the chocolate mixture and the sifted icing sugar until well blended and smooth. Chill until firm enough to spread easily.
9 Use a long serrated knife to cut the cool cake in half horizontally. Use about a quarter of the chocolate crème to sandwich the halves together, then spread half the remaining mixture over the top and sides of the cake.
10 Chill the remaining icing until firm, which will take 1 to 2 hours. Scoop teaspoonfuls on to a saucer and roll in cocoa powder or icing sugar until smooth and round like truffles. They will be quite soft and really need to be chilled overnight if you have time. Arrange on top of the cake. Dust with cocoa powder or decorate with chocolate curls, if you like.

Cook's Tip
If you are in a hurry, skip step 9 and decorate the cake instead with just a little sifted cocoa powder and grated chocolate. Or, just sprinkle the cake halves with Amaretti liqueur and dust with icing sugar.

CAPPUCCINO SWIRL

Time to make: 15 minutes
Time to bake: 45 to 55 minutes
Makes an 18 cm (7 in) round cake that cuts into 8 slices

2 tablespoons instant coffee granules
125 g (4 oz) sunflower margarine
½ teaspoon vanilla essence
125 g (4 oz) caster sugar
1 egg, size 3
2 tablespoons golden syrup
250 g (8 oz) self-raising flour
4 tablespoons milk

Cappuccino Cream Icing
60 g (2 oz) plain chocolate
30 g (1 oz) butter, at room temperature
155 ml (5 fl oz) double cream
30 g (1 oz) icing sugar

Storing and Freezing
Store the un-iced cake for up to 5 days in a cake tin; the cake should ideally be eaten the day it is iced, although it will keep for 1 or 2 days in the fridge.

Freeze the un-iced cake for up to 3 months in a plastic bag or an airtight container. Defrost for 4 hours at room temperature.

I like to serve this cream and chocolate swirled cake with its strong coffee flavour for elevenses with a cup of frothy cappuccino coffee or with strong, black after-dinner coffee as a dessert. As I'm sure you've guessed, I have based this cake on the flavours of Italian cappuccino coffee, which is drunk in every cafe and wine bar in town.

1 Set the oven to 180C, 350F, Gas 4. Grease an 18 cm (7 in) round deep cake tin and line the base with greaseproof paper.
2 Dissolve the coffee in a large bowl with 2 tablespoons hot water. Add the margarine, vanilla, sugar, egg, golden syrup, flour and milk and beat until the mixture is light and fluffy.
3 Spread the mixture into the prepared tin and level the top. Bake in the centre of the oven for 45 to 55 minutes until firm to the touch. Allow the cake to cool in the tin for 10 minutes, then turn it out on to a wire rack, peel off the lining paper and leave to cool completely; it may sink slightly in the centre but this allows a good depth of icing on top.
4 To make the cappuccino cream icing, break the chocolate into a bowl over a saucepan of simmering water and stir until it melts. (Or, melt in a microwave on High for 1½ to 2 minutes.) Remove from the heat and set aside to cool slightly. Stir in the butter until melted.
5 Put the cream into a bowl and whip until it forms soft peaks, then stir in the sugar. Swirl the chocolate into the cream but do not over-mix or you will loose the marbled look. Swirl the icing over the top of the cake.

Cook's Tip

If you have an espresso machine, use 2 tablespoons of strong espresso coffee or dissolve instant coffee in water. If you like, spoon a little coffee-flavoured liqueur over the cake before adding the icing.

CHOCOLATE FRUIT AND NUT CAKE

Time to make: 50 minutes
Time to bake: 1½ to 1¾ hours
Makes an 18 cm (7 in) square cake that cuts into 15 slices, or a 20 cm (8 in) round cake that cuts into 12 slices

125 g (4 oz) jar maraschino cherries
185 g (6 oz) ready-to-eat dried apricots, chopped
125 g (4 oz) ready-to-eat dried figs, chopped
125 g (4 oz) ready-to-eat dried dates, chopped
125 g (4 oz) butter, softened
125 g (4 oz) caster sugar
60 g (2 oz) cocoa powder
185 g (6 oz) plain flour
4 eggs, size 3, lightly beaten
315 g (10 oz) mixed whole shelled nuts

Decorations

3 tablespoons apricot jam
icing sugar, for dusting
750 g (1½ lb) white almond paste
cocoa powder, for dusting

Storing and Freezing
Store for up to 1 month in a cake tin.
Freeze the un-iced cake for up to 2 months in a plastic bag or an airtight container. Defrost for 12 hours at room temperature, then ice.

Chocolate Fruit and Nut Cake

After about 15 years of working on Christmas features for various magazines I wanted to do something different, so I developed this cake as an alternative Christmas cake. It is choc-a-bloc full of nuts, dried apricots and fruits with just a little cake mixture to bind everything together. Use maraschino cherries if you can because they're a lovely moist surprise in the mouth.

For a really festive look I wrap the cake in almond paste and shape a strip of almond paste into a bow, but an equally attractive finish is just to top it with yet more fruit and nuts.

1 Set the oven to 180C, 350F, Gas 4. Grease an 18 cm (7 in) deep square or a 20 cm (8 in) round deep cake tin and line the base and sides with a double layer of greaseproof paper, see page 11. Drain the maraschino cherries, reserving the syrup.
2 Put the cherries, apricots, figs and dates into a bowl and set aside. Put the butter and sugar into a bowl and cream together until light and fluffy. Sift the cocoa powder and flour together, then fold into the creamed mixture alternately with the eggs.
3 Stir the cherries, figs, apricots, dates and nuts into the cake mixture with 2 tablespoons of the cherry syrup and mix together.
4 Spread the mixture in the tin and level. Bake for 1½ to 1¾ hours until firm to the touch. Leave to cool completely in the tin on a wire rack, then peel off the lining paper.
5 When the cake is cool, put the apricot jam into a small pan over a low heat and stir until it begins to melt. Press the jam through a fine sieve. Brush the top and sides of the cake with the apricot jam, then position the cake on a 23 cm (9 in) cake board.
6 Dust a dry work surface with icing sugar. Reserve about 150 g (5 oz) of almond paste, then roll out the remainder into a 28 cm (11 in) square or a 33 cm (13 in) circle large enough to cover the top and sides of the cake. Drape the almond paste over the cake, smoothing the top and sides with the palms of your hands.
7 Trim off the excess almond paste and roll the trimmings together with the reserved almond paste into 5 long strips. Trim the strips to about 2.5 cm (1 in) wide. Arrange 4 strips over the cake like ribbons, then shape a bow with the last strip. Dust the top of the cake with cocoa powder.

CHOCOLATE CHESTNUT ROULADE

Time to make: 35 minutes
Time to bake: 15 to 20 minutes
Makes a roulade that cuts into 8 to 10 slices

125 g (4 oz) plain chocolate
4 eggs, size 3, separated
125 g (4 oz) caster sugar, plus a little extra for sprinkling

Chestnut Filling

315 ml (10 fl oz) double cream
250 g (8 oz) canned natural chestnut purée
4 tablespoons icing sugar
1 to 2 tablespoons brandy

Decoration

icing sugar, to dust
8 marrons glacé

Storing and Freezing
Store for up to 3 days in the fridge. Freeze for up to 1 month in a plastic bag or an airtight container. Defrost for 5 to 6 hours in the fridge.

Photographed on page 27

Even though this is more of a pudding than a cake, I didn't think this book would be complete without the ultimate roulade. I often make this for large family gatherings as the cake is made a day ahead and can be rolled up with the filling and put into the fridge three to four hours before serving, which means I have plenty of time to get ready. It is perfect for wedding buffets, too, as everyone seems to love it. Simply fill the roulade with whipped cream and fresh raspberries, or try my favourite filling with chestnut purée, which I include here.

1 Set the oven to 180C, 350F, Gas 4. Grease a 27 × 33 cm (11 × 13 in) Swiss roll tin and line the base and sides with greaseproof paper, see page 11.
2 Break the chocolate into a heatproof bowl over a pan of gently simmering water and stir until it melts. (Or, melt in a microwave on High for 2 to 3 minutes.) Remove from the heat.
3 Put the egg yolks and sugar into a bowl and whisk for about 5 minutes until pale and creamy; they will not increase in volume a great deal. Stir the melted chocolate into the egg yolk mixture.
4 Put the egg whites into a clean grease-free bowl and whisk until they form stiff peaks. Use a large metal spoon to beat 2 tablespoons into the mixture, then fold in the remainder.
5 Spread mixture in the prepared tin and level the top. Bake in the centre of the oven for 15 to 20 minutes until risen and firm; the cake will have a crust on top and appear to be uncooked underneath, but this is correct.
6 While the cake is baking, sprinkle a sheet of greaseproof paper at least as large as the cake with caster sugar. As soon as the cake comes out of the oven turn it out on to the paper, then carefully peel off the lining paper. Use a sharp knife to trim off all the crisp edges. Cover with another sheet of greaseproof paper and a clean damp tea towel. Allow the cake to cool completely.
7 Meanwhile, to make the chestnut filling, put the cream into a bowl and whip it until it just holds it's shape. Spoon about 5 tablespoons for decoration into a small bowl and set aside. Put the chestnut purée, icing sugar and brandy into a bowl and beat

CHOCOLATE CHESTNUT ROULADE

Time to make: 35 minutes
Time to bake: 15 to 20 minutes
Makes a roulade that cuts into 8 to 10 slices

125 g (4 oz) plain chocolate
4 eggs, size 3, separated
125 g (4 oz) caster sugar, plus a little extra for sprinkling

Chestnut Filling

315 ml (10 fl oz) double cream
250 g (8 oz) canned natural chestnut purée
4 tablespoons icing sugar
1 to 2 tablespoons brandy

Decoration

icing sugar, to dust
8 marrons glacé

Storing and Freezing
Store for up to 3 days in the fridge.
Freeze for up to 1 month in a plastic bag or an airtight container. Defrost for 5 to 6 hours in the fridge.

Photographed on page 27

Even though this is more of a pudding than a cake, I didn't think this book would be complete without the ultimate roulade. I often make this for large family gatherings as the cake is made a day ahead and can be rolled up with the filling and put into the fridge three to four hours before serving, which means I have plenty of time to get ready. It is perfect for wedding buffets, too, as everyone seems to love it. Simply fill the roulade with whipped cream and fresh raspberries, or try my favourite filling with chestnut purée, which I include here.

1 Set the oven to 180C, 350F, Gas 4. Grease a 27 × 33 cm (11 × 13 in) Swiss roll tin and line the base and sides with greaseproof paper, see page 11.
2 Break the chocolate into a heatproof bowl over a pan of gently simmering water and stir until it melts. (Or, melt in a microwave on High for 2 to 3 minutes.) Remove from the heat.
3 Put the egg yolks and sugar into a bowl and whisk for about 5 minutes until pale and creamy; they will not increase in volume a great deal. Stir the melted chocolate into the egg yolk mixture.
4 Put the egg whites into a clean grease-free bowl and whisk until they form stiff peaks. Use a large metal spoon to beat 2 tablespoons into the mixture, then fold in the remainder.
5 Spread mixture in the prepared tin and level the top. Bake in the centre of the oven for 15 to 20 minutes until risen and firm; the cake will have a crust on top and appear to be uncooked underneath, but this is correct.
6 While the cake is baking, sprinkle a sheet of greaseproof paper at least as large as the cake with caster sugar. As soon as the cake comes out of the oven turn it out on to the paper, then carefully peel off the lining paper. Use a sharp knife to trim off all the crisp edges. Cover with another sheet of greaseproof paper and a clean damp tea towel. Allow the cake to cool completely.
7 Meanwhile, to make the chestnut filling, put the cream into a bowl and whip it until it just holds it's shape. Spoon about 5 tablespoons for decoration into a small bowl and set aside. Put the chestnut purée, icing sugar and brandy into a bowl and beat

together until well blended and smooth, then fold in the whipped cream. Refrigerate if not using immediately.
8 Remove the tea towel and top sheet of greaseproof paper from the cake. Spread the chestnut filling over the cake and roll up from one short end, using the bottom sheet of greaseproof paper to help you lift and roll it. The cake will crack, but this looks very effective and is actually how it should be. Shower with sifted icing sugar.
9 Arrange spoonfuls of the remaining whipped cream over the top of the cake, then decorate with marrons glacé.

Cook's Tip
When you turn out the cake and cover it with the tea towel it can be left overnight before it is filled. Just keep it tightly covered so it doesn't dry out.

Chocolate Leaves
Sometimes I decorate this roulade with chocolate leaves, as well as marrons glacé. To make chocolate leaves, paint melted chocolate on to the undersides of rose leaves, bay leaves or holly leaves. Leave to set. Repeat if necessary, then peel off the leaves.

CHOCOLATE WHISKY CAKE

Time to make: 50 minutes
Time to bake: 55 minutes
Makes a 20 cm (8 in) round cake that cuts into 8 slices

250 g (8 oz) plain chocolate
185 g (6 oz) unsalted butter, at room temperature
185 g (6 oz) caster sugar
5 eggs, size 3, lightly beaten and at room temperature
125 g (4 oz) self-raising flour
2 tablespoons whisky
60 g (2 oz) milk chocolate, to decorate

Filling

4 tablespoons whisky
6 tablespoons apricot jam

Rich Chocolate Icing

185 g (6 oz) plain chocolate
90 g (3 oz) butter
90 ml (3 fl oz) double cream

Storing and Freezing
Store for up to 6 days in a cake tin.
Freeze the un-iced cake in a plastic bag or an airtight container for up to 1 month. Defrost for 5 to 6 hours at room temperature, then ice.

Chocolate Whisky Cake (front) with Chocolate Chestnut Roulade, see page 24

This moist cake flavoured with whisky is the perfect gift for Father's Day. I guarantee it will be appreciated by any man because of it's strong dark flavour. My father and husband have both been happy recipients. But, of course, it would be equally welcome if given to a woman on Valentine's Day. Pipe an appropriate message on top in milk chocolate and hide in a box until the day!

1 Set the oven to 180C, 350F, Gas 4. Grease a 20 cm (8 in) round deep or springform cake tin and line the base with greaseproof paper.
2 Break the chocolate into a heatproof bowl over a saucepan of simmering water and stir until it melts. (Or, melt in the microwave on High for 2 to 3 minutes.)
3 Put the butter and sugar into a bowl and cream together until light and fluffy. Gradually beat in the eggs, adding a little of the flour if the mixture begins to curdle. Sift over the remaining flour, then fold it in along with the melted chocolate and the 2 tablespoons whisky.
4 Spread the mixture into the prepared tin and level the top. Bake in the centre of the oven for 55 minutes or until firm to the touch. Allow the cake to cool in the tin for 10 minutes, then turn it out on to a wire rack, peel off the lining paper and leave to cool completely.
5 Use a long serrated knife to split the cooled cake in half, then sprinkle with 4 tablespoons whisky. Sandwich the halves with jam.
6 To make the rich chocolate icing, break the chocolate into a heatproof bowl over a saucepan of simmering water and stir until it melts. (Or, melt in a microwave on High for 3 minutes.) Remove the bowl from the heat and stir in the butter and cream until smooth. Pour over top and sides of cake, smooth it evenly down the sides with a palette knife.
7 Break the milk chocolate into a heatproof bowl over a pan of simmering water and stir until it melts. (Or, melt in a microwave on High for 1½ to 2 minutes.) Place the chocolate into a greaseproof paper piping bag, snip off the end and pipe zig-zags or a message on top of the cake.

CHOC AND GINGER RING

Time to make: 25 minutes
Time to bake: 55 minutes to 1 hour
Makes a ring cake that cuts into 10 slices

125 g (4 oz) ginger biscuits
125 g (4 oz) plain chocolate
125 g (4 oz) butter, softened
185 g (6 oz) caster sugar
2 eggs, size 3, at room temperature
1 teaspoon vanilla essence
250 g (8 oz) plain flour
1 teaspoon baking powder
1 teaspoon bicarbonate of soda
2 teaspoons ground ginger
315 ml (10 fl oz) soured cream
60 g (2 oz) milk chocolate, to decorate

Chocolate Brandy Icing

155 g (5 oz) plain chocolate
125 g (4 oz) butter
2 tablespoons brandy

Storing and Freezing
Store for up to 4 days in a cool place; the fridge temperature will set the icing, but I think this makes the texture too firm and the cake loses its flavour, so store it in a cake tin and enjoy the sticky icing.

Open freeze until the icing is firm, then freeze for up to 1 month in a plastic bag or in an airtight container. Defrost for 3 to 4 hours at room temperature.

If you like the combination of chocolate and ginger as much as I do, this cake will become a favourite. A packet of ginger biscuits lasts for only 2 days in my house, so I only buy them as a rare treat – but they were definitely the inspiration for this cake. With its unusual flavouring of ginger biscuits and grated chocolate and dark icing, this is very rich and ideal for entertaining.

1 Set the oven to 180C, 350F, Gas 4. Thickly butter and flour a 1.25 litre (2½ pint) ring tin, tapping out any excess flour.
2 Place the biscuits into a thick paper or plastic bag, seal the bag closed and bang with the end of a rolling pin until crushed, then set aside. Finely chop the chocolate and set aside.
3 Put the butter and sugar into a bowl and cream together until light and fluffy. Gradually beat in the eggs and vanilla essence, adding a little of the flour if the mixture begins to curdle. Sift over the remaining flour, the baking powder, bicarbonate of soda and ginger together, then use a large metal spoon to fold them in along with the soured cream.
4 Spread half the mixture in the tin, then use the back of a spoon to make a hollow channel all the way round. Sprinkle the biscuits and chocolate into the channel, then spread the remaining cake mixture over and level the top. Bake in the centre of the oven for 55 minutes to 1 hour until golden and firm. Allow the cake to cool in the tin for 10 minutes, then turn it out on to a wire rack to cool completely.
5 To make the chocolate brandy icing, break the chocolate into a small saucepan over a low heat. Add the butter and brandy and stir until the chocolate melts and the mixture is well blended and smooth. Remove from the heat and set aside to cool until it will thickly coat the back of a spoon. If you are in a hurry, chill the mixture in the fridge. Pour the icing evenly over the cake, spreading down over the sides until they are coated.
6 Break the milk chocolate into a small heatproof bowl over a saucepan of simmering water and stir until it melts. (Or, melt in a microwave on High for 1½ to 2 minutes.) Place in a greaseproof paper piping bag, snip off the end and drizzle chocolate over the top of the cake.

WHITE CHOCOLATE WEDDING CAKE

Time to make: allow 3 days
Time to bake: up to 1½ hours
Makes a three-tier cake to serve 50 guests

625 g (1¼ lb) butter, at room temperature
625 g (1¼ lb) caster sugar
10 eggs, size 3, lightly beaten
625 g (1¼ lb) self-raising flour
315 g (10 oz) plain flour
finely grated rind of 3 lemons
185 g (6 oz) white chocolate dots
6 tablespoons brandy

White Chocolate Ganache

470 g (15 oz) white chocolate
90 g (3 oz) unsalted butter
3 tablespoons brandy
940 ml (1½ pints) double cream

Decoration

450 g (1 lb) white chocolate
fresh flowers, such as roses, freesias, gypsophilia, cornflowers, or fresh fruit, such as strings of redcurrants, strawberries, raspberries, cape gooseberries and sliced peaches

So many brides now ask for a chocolate wedding cake instead of the traditional rich fruit cake. This wonderful cake was developed by Joanna Farrow for a wedding buffet in *BBC Good Food* magazine. It looks spectacular, wrapped in white chocolate ruffles and decorated with fresh flowers, and tastes delicious. I think it would be equally good made with dark chocolate, too.

The secret to the decorating is to wrap the chocolate ruffle around the cake while the chocolate is still pliable but just set and while the cake is still partly frozen; you will need an empty fridge. But if you find this too complicated, simply make a little extra ganache to pipe around the edges, and decorate with fresh flowers, but be sure you remove them before serving.

1 Set the oven to 160C, 325F, Gas 3. Grease 3 round deep cakes tins measuring 15 cm (6 in), 20 cm (8 in) and 25 cm (10 in) and line the bases and sides with greaseproof paper.
2 Put the butter and sugar into a bowl and cream together until light and fluffy. Gradually beat in the eggs, adding a little of the flour if the mixture begins to curdle. Sift both flours together over the creamed mixture and use a large metal spoon to fold them in along with the lemon rind and chocolate dots.
3 Divide the mixture evenly between the prepared tins and level the tops. Bake for 50 minutes for the 15 cm (6 in) cake, 1 to 1¼ hours for the 20 cm (8 in) cake and about 1½ hours for the 25 cm (10 in) cake. Each cake should be firm to the touch and a skewer inserted in the centre should come out clean. Leave the cakes to cool in the tins for 5 minutes, then turn them out on to wire racks, peel off the lining papers and leave then to cool.
4 Pierce the cool cakes all over with a cocktail stick and sprinkle over the brandy and allow it to soak in. Place each cake on a large square of non-stick baking parchment.
5 Make the white chocolate ganache for the icing in 3 batches for the best results; break 155 g (5 oz) of the white chocolate into a small heatproof bowl over a saucepan of gently simmering water, add 30 g (1 oz) of the butter and 1 tablespoon brandy and

Continued on page 30

White Chocolate Wedding Cake continued from page 29

Note
Flowers are for decoration only – remove before serving, and take care that you do not use any poisonous plants.

Variation
To make a one-tier white chocolate celebration cake, like the one in the photograph, bake and decorate the 25 cm (10 in) tier. You will need 315 g (10 oz) butter, 315 g (10 oz) caster sugar, 5 eggs (size 3), 315 g (10 oz) self-raising flour, 155g (5 oz) plain flour, finely grated rind of 2 lemons, 90 g (3 oz) white chocolate dots, and 2 tablespoons brandy.

Prepare the mixture as in step 2 and bake for about 1½ hours until the cake is firm to the touch and a skewer inserted in the centre comes out clean.

Make up half the quantity of the White Chocolate Ganache on page 29 for the decoration.

White Chocolate Wedding Cake

stir until the white chocolate melts. (Or, melt in a microwave on High for 2 to 3 minutes.) Remove from the heat and leave to cool slightly. Put 315 ml (10 fl oz) of the cream into a bowl and whisk until it just holds its shape, then stir it into the white chocolate. Spread it over the top and sides of the 20 cm (8 in) tier. Make another batch of icing and spread it over the 15 cm (6 in) tier, saving any extra to add to the final portion so you have enough for the 25 cm (10 in) tier. At this point, you can open freeze the cakes until the icing is firm, then freeze them for up to 1 month in a plastic bag or an airtight container.

6 To decorate, 2 days before the wedding, remove the cakes from the freezer but do not allow them to defrost. Cut out 3 strips of greaseproof paper long enough to wrap around each cake and wide enough to stand 2.5 cm (1 in) above the top of each. Cut a wavy scalloped edge along one side of each strip and place it flat on a work surface.

7 Break the remaining 185g (6 oz) white chocolate into a heatproof bowl over a saucepan of gently simmering water and stir until it melts. Spread the melted chocolate evenly over the greaseproof papers and allow to cool until just beginning to set, but is not hard.

8 Place the largest cake on a 30 cm (12 in) cake board, then stack the cakes one on top of the other while still frozen. Starting with the top tier, wrap the strip of greaseproof paper around the cake, chocolate side against the cake and pressing gently on to the icing. Leave for 5 to 10 minutes and the cold of the frozen cakes will help the chocolate set. Once hardened, peel away the paper. Repeat on the other tiers. Store the cake in the fridge until completely thawed and ready to serve.

9 Two to 3 hours before serving, decorate the top with fresh flowers or fruit and wrap a pretty ribbon around the side, if you like. Leave in a cool place until ready to cut.

Cook's Tip
On a warm sunny day it is important to keep the cake chilled as the icing will melt quickly.

SACHERTORTE

Time to make: 40 minutes, plus 30 minutes for the icing
Time to bake: 50 minutes to 1 hour
Makes a 20 cm (8 in) round cake that cuts into 8 slices

155 g (5 oz) dark chocolate
155 g (5 oz) butter, at room temperature
155 g (5 oz) icing sugar
5 eggs, size 3, separated, at room temperature
155 g (5 oz) self-raising flour
30 g (1 oz) cornflour
1 tablespoon dark rum
5 tablespoons apricot jam
60 g (2 oz) milk chocolate, to decorate

Chocolate Glaze Icing

125 g (4 oz) caster sugar
155 g (5 oz) plain chocolate

Storing and Freezing
Store for up to 1 week in a cake tin.
Freeze the un-filled and un-iced cake for up to 3 months in a plastic bag or an airtight container. Defrost for 4 to 5 hours at room temperature before filling and icing.

One year I went to Vienna for a weekend at the end of November to do all my present shopping in the Austrian Christmas markets. It's exhausting work shopping, so I stopped frequently for a slice of Sachertorte and a pot of coffee. Plus, of course, I had to make stops for warming *gluhwein*.

This is the most authentic recipe for Sachertorte that I have made. Sprinkled with rum and filled with apricot jam, this moist rich cake is as good as any slice you could buy in an Austrian coffeehouse. The icing is tricky to make but I think well worth the effort for a glossy smooth result. If you don't feel confident about trying the icing, however, don't let it put you off making such a wonderful cake. Instead, use one of the simpler icings in this chapter, such as the one for Chocolate Whisky Cake on page 26.

1 Set the oven to 150C, 300F, Gas 2. Grease a 20 cm (8 in) round deep or springform cake tin and line the base with greaseproof paper.
2 Break the chocolate into a heatproof bowl over a saucepan of simmering water, add 1 tablespoon warm water and stir until the chocolate melts. (Or, melt the chocolate with 1 tablespoon warm water in a microwave on High for 1 to 2 minutes.) Remove the bowl from the heat and set aside to cool slightly.
3 Put the butter and sugar into a bowl and cream together until light and fluffy, then gradually beat in the melted chocolate. Gradually beat the egg yolks into the creamed mixture, adding a little flour if it begins to curdle. Sift the remaining flour and the cornflour over, then use a large metal spoon to fold in.
4 Put the egg whites into a clean grease-free bowl and whisk until they form soft peaks. Beat 1 tablespoon of the egg white into the cake mixture, then use a large metal spoon to carefully fold in the remainder.
5 Spread the mixture in the prepared tin and level the top. Bake in the centre of the oven for 50 minutes to 1 hour until firm to the touch. As soon as the cake is baked, turn it out on to a wire rack, peel off the lining paper and allow it to cool.
6 Meanwhile, put the apricot jam into a small saucepan over a

low heat and stir until it begins to melt. (Or, melt in a microwave on High for about 30 seconds.) Press the jam through a sieve.

7 Use a serrated knife to cut the cool cake in half horizontally. Sprinkle both halves with rum, then use 2 tablespoons apricot jam to sandwich together. Spread the remaining jam over the top and sides of the cake, then place the cake on a wire rack.

8 To make the chocolate glaze icing, put the sugar and 155 ml (5 fl oz) water in a saucepan over a low heat and stir to dissolve the sugar, then bring to the boil without stirring and continue boiling until the mixture reaches 115C, 240F on a sugar thermometer, the soft ball stage (see Cook's Tip). Remove the pan from the heat.

9 Break the plain chocolate into a large heatproof bowl over a pan of simmering water, add 3 tablespoons water and stir until the chocolate melts. (Or, melt the chocolate and water in a microwave on High for 1 to 2 minutes.) Using an electric hand-held whisk, pour the sugar syrup in a thin stream on to the chocolate, beating constantly to give a coating consistency. Pour the icing over the cake and spread it down over the sides with a palette knife. Lift the cake immediately on to the serving plate or the icing will wrinkle and crack when moved.

10 Break the milk chocolate into a heatproof bowl over a pan of simmering water and stir until it melts. (Or, melt in a microwave on High for 1½ to 2 minutes.) Place the melted chocolate into a small greaseproof piping bag and cut off the tip. Pipe the name Sachertorte across the top of the cake.

Cook's Tip

A sugar thermometer is invaluable for getting the sugar syrup to the correct temperature but not essential. If you don't have one, drop a teaspoon of the mixture into a bowl of cold water. When it forms a soft ball it is ready to use.

TIRAMISU CAKE

Time to make: 40 minutes
Time to bake: 35 minutes
Makes a 22 cm (8½ in) round cake that cuts into 8 slices

1 tablespoon instant coffee granules
60 g (2 oz) plain chocolate
125 g (4 oz) self-raising flour
1 teaspoon baking powder
125 g (4 oz) sunflower margarine
125 g (4 oz) caster sugar
2 eggs, size 3, lightly beaten
4 tablespoons brandy, or chocolate- or coffee-flavoured liqueur
cocoa powder, to dust

Tiramisu Icing

250 g (8 oz) mascarpone cheese
2 tablespoons icing sugar
3 tablespoons single cream or milk

Storing and Freezing
Store for up to 3 days in the fridge, however the cake is best iced on the day it is to be served as the icing has a tendency to dry out and look a bit sad. Once iced, store the cake in an airtight polythene box in the fridge.

Freeze the un-iced cake for up to 3 months in a plastic bag or an airtight container. Defrost for 3 to 4 hours at room temperature, then ice.

Tiramisu Cake

I adore Italian tiramisu but it is in danger of becoming the 90s version of trifle, so I've combined the flavours to create this ultimate indulgence that is a bit more elegant. This is ideal as a dinner party dessert or a very special cake for a party. If you prefer a simpler presentation, just slice the cake and serve the mascarpone on the side of the plate and dust it with a little cocoa powder.

1 Set the oven to 160C, 325F, Gas 3. Grease a 22 cm (8½ in) round deep or springform cake tin and line the base with greaseproof paper. Dissolve the coffee granules in 1 teaspoon hot water and set aside.
2 Coarsely grate the chocolate into a mixing bowl, then add the flour, baking powder, sunflower margarine, sugar, eggs and dissolved coffee. Beat well with a wooden spoon for 1 to 2 minutes until well blended and smooth.
3 Spread the mixture in the prepared tin and level the top. Bake in centre of the oven for 35 minutes or until firm to the touch. Allow the cake to cool in the tin for 5 minutes, then turn it out on to a wire rack, peel off the lining paper and leave to cool completely.
4 Place the cooled cake upside down and spoon the brandy or liqueur over the top, allowing it to soak in for 10 minutes before icing. Place the cake the right way up on a serving plate.
5 To make the tiramisu icing, put the mascarpone cheese, sifted icing sugar and cream or milk into a bowl and beat together until well blended and smooth. Spread over the top of the cake. Dust thickly with cocoa powder.

WHITE CHOCOLATE FLAKE GÂTEAU

Time to make: 45 minutes
Time to bake: 1¼ to 1½ hours
Makes a 20 cm (8 in) round cake that cuts into 11 to 12 slices

250 ml (8 fl oz) milk
1 tablespoon white wine vinegar
125 g (4 oz) plain chocolate
345 g (11 oz) self-raising flour
15 g (½ oz) cocoa powder
1 teaspoon bicarbonate of soda
125 g (4 oz) sunflower margarine
250 g (8 oz) golden caster sugar
2 eggs, size 3
4 tablespoons sweet sherry
icing sugar, to dust

Chocolate Curls

125 g (4 oz) white chocolate
125 g (4 oz) white chocolate-flavour cake covering

Filling and Icing

625 ml (1 pint) double cream
4 tablespoons icing sugar

I think this is the perfect cake to make for a special occasion such as an adult's birthday. Why not take one into the office next time there is a celebration? This is a large cake and will easily feed 12 hungry friends. Make the cake in advance and fill and ice it on the day of serving.

I discovered the secret of making the chocolate curls from a recipe used by the bakers at Patisserie Valerie in London's Soho. They are easy to make, but you must use a blend of chocolate-flavour cake covering and good-quality chocolate or the mixture will be too brittle to curl easily.

1 Set the oven to 160C, 325F, Gas 3. Grease a 20 cm (8 in) round deep or springform cake tin and line the base and sides with greaseproof paper.
2 Measure the milk into a measuring jug, then stir in the vinegar; do not worry if it curdles. Break the chocolate into a heatproof bowl over a saucepan of simmering water and stir until it melts. (Or, melt in the microwave on High for 1½ to 2 minutes.)
3 Sift the flour, cocoa powder and bicarbonate of soda into a bowl. Add the margarine, sugar, eggs and half of the milk mixture and beat together. Beat in the melted chocolate and the remaining milk mixture, beating until well blended and smooth.
4 Spread the mixture into the prepared tin and level the top. Bake in the centre of the oven for 1¼ to 1½ hours until firm to the touch and a skewer inserted in the centre comes out clean. Allow the cake to cool completely in the tin, then turn it out on to a wire rack, peel off the lining paper and leave it to cool.
5 Meanwhile, make the chocolate curls. Break the white chocolate and cake covering into a heatproof bowl over a saucepan of simmering water and stir until they melt. (Or, melt in a microwave on High for 3 to 4 minutes.) Pour the melted chocolate mixture into a clean, dry margarine tub or plastic carton and allow to set; it needs to be about 2.5 cm (1 in) thick.
6 When the mixture is set, turn it out and use a potato peeler to shave off thin curls.
7 Use a long serrated knife to cut the cool cake in half

Storing and Freezing
Store the un-filled and un-iced cake for up to 4 days in a cake tin. Once filled and iced, store for 1 to 2 days in the fridge.

Freeze the un-filled and un-iced cake for up to 3 months in a plastic bag or an airtight container. Defrost for 8 hours at room temperature.

horizontally, then sprinkle the cut sides with sherry.

8 To make the filling and icing, put the cream into a bowl and sift over the icing sugar, then whip until the cream just holds its shape. Use one-third to sandwich the halves together, then place the cake on a serving plate. Spread the remaining whipped cream over the top and the sides of the cake.

9 Make sure your hands are cool and carefully arrange the chocolate curls all over the top and sides of the cake. Dust the top of the cake with icing sugar.

Variation

When cherries are at their peak and plentiful in summer, fill the cake with fresh stoned cherries, sprinkle with kirsch instead of sherry and top with a few cherries on their stalks, too.

Cook's Tip

Be sure you use a high fat sunflower margarine that is suitable for baking. Low-fat margarines contain too much water for successful results.

ITALIAN BISCUIT CAKE

Time to make: 20 minutes
Time to chill: 1 hour
Makes a 500 g (1 lb) loaf that cuts into 10 slices

125 g (4 oz) Amaretti biscuits

60 g (2 oz) stem ginger, well drained

90 g (3 oz) ready-to-eat dried apricots

125 g (4 oz) plain chocolate

1 tablespoon golden syrup

125 g (4 oz) butter

60 g (2 oz) natural-coloured glacé cherries

60 g (2 oz) raisins

60 g (2 oz) hazelnuts

Storing and Freezing
Store for up to 2 weeks in the fridge.
Freeze for up to 1 month. Defrost for 6 hours in the fridge.

This is a wickedly rich, no-bake treat that is very quick and simple to make, and then it just sets in the fridge until you are ready to serve it. Once cut, however, I dare you not to nibble a slice every time you open the fridge door!

1 Line a 500 g (1 lb) loaf tin with cling film, leaving a large enough overhang on the sides to fold up over the top. Roughly crush the Amaretti biscuits and set aside. Chop the ginger and apricots and set aside.
2 Break the chocolate into a saucepan over a medium heat, add the golden syrup and butter and stir until the chocolate and butter melt and everything is well blended.
3 Stir the crushed Amaretti biscuits, chopped ginger, apricots, cherries, raisins and hazelnuts into the pan.
4 Pack the chocolate mixture into the prepared tin and level the top. Fold up the excess cling film and put in the fridge to set for at least 1 hour. To serve, invert on to a serving plate and peel of the cling film. Cut into thin slices.

Variations
You can vary the type of fruits, nuts and biscuits, or leave out the ginger according to taste. For a family version, use digestive biscuits and increase the raisin and cherry quantities to make up the same total weight of fruit.

Italian Biscuit Cake

PRUNE AND CHOCOLATE CAKE

Time to make: 35 minutes
Time to bake: 20 minutes
Makes a 28 × 18 cm (11 × 7 in) cake that cuts into 12 pieces

155 g (5 oz) stoned prunes
3 egg whites, size 2
1 teaspoon vanilla essence
155 g (5 oz) plain flour
220 g (7 oz) caster sugar
90 g (3 oz) cocoa powder
1½ teaspoons baking powder
¼ teaspoon bicarbonate of soda
¼ teaspoon salt

Quick Cocoa Icing

155 g (5 oz) icing sugar
15 g (½ oz) cocoa powder
1 tablespoon skimmed milk

Storing and Freezing
Store for up to 1 week in a cake tin.
Freeze for up to 1 month in a plastic bag or an airtight container. Defrost for about 1 hour at room temperature.

This fat-free cake was developed by the Californian Prune Board for promotional purposes, but don't let that put you off because it is actually very good. In fact, Lydia, my tester, and her young daughter loved it. The prune purée provides the moistness, natural sweetness and what I call 'mouth feel' that I think you need in a cake. The cake is also loaded with fibre, iron, vitamin A and potassium, and as there isn't any butter or margarine in it there's no cholesterol and fewer calories than you would expect in a cake. So you can have your cake and eat it, too – without feeling guilty!

The icing is quite dark and strongly cocoa flavoured, so if you prefer, just dust the top with icing sugar and serve with crème fraîche, but don't forget the calories you are adding then!

1 Set the oven to 180C, 350F, Gas 4. Grease a 28 × 18 cm (11 × 7 in) Swiss roll tin and line the base with greaseproof paper.
2 Place the prunes and 3 tablespoons water into a food processor or blender and whizz to make a smooth purée. Place the purée, egg whites, vanilla essence and 250 ml (8 fl oz) water into a bowl and beat until well blended, then sift in the flour, sugar, cocoa powder, baking powder, bicarbonate of soda and salt and stir until well blended.
3 Spread the mixture in the prepared tin. Bake in the centre of the oven for 20 minutes or until firm to the touch. Allow the cake to cool completely in the tin on a wire rack.
4 To make the quick cocoa icing, sift the icing sugar and cocoa powder into a bowl, then stir in the milk until the icing is well blended and smooth.
5 Turn out the cooled cake, peel off the lining paper and spread the icing over the top.

COCONUT BOUNTY CAKE

Time to make: 30 minutes
Time to bake: 45 to 50 minutes
Makes an 18 cm (7 in) round cake that cuts into 10 slices

2 egg whites, size 3
125 g (4 oz) caster sugar
90 g (3 oz) desiccated coconut
185 g (6 oz) golden syrup
90 g (3 oz) butter
125 g (4 oz) plain flour
60 g (2 oz) cocoa powder
½ teaspoon bicarbonate of soda
2 eggs, size 3, lightly beaten and at room temperature
2 tablespoons milk

Coconut Icing

30 g (1 oz) instant coconut milk powder
90 g (3 oz) icing sugar
1 tablespoon boiling water

Storing and Freezing
Store for up to 5 days in a cake tin. Freeze for up to 2 months in a plastic bag or an airtight container. Defrost for 5 to 6 hours at room temperature.

I went to tea with some friends and they served me an amazing cake filled with coconut icing, which came from *The Sainsbury Collection: Cakes and Baking.* I have adapted the recipe to make this chocolate version.

1 Set the oven to 160C, 325F, Gas 3. Grease an 18 cm (7 in) round deep or springform cake tin and line the base with greaseproof paper.
2 Place the egg whites, 90 g (3 oz) of the caster sugar and the coconut into a saucepan over a low heat and heat, stirring, for about 5 minutes until the sugar dissolves; be very careful that the mixture does not catch and burn. Reserve 1 tablespoon of this coconut mixture for decoration.
3 Place the golden syrup, remaining sugar and the butter in another pan over medium heat and heat, stirring occasionally, until the sugar dissolves and the butter melts.
4 Sift the flour, cocoa and bicarbonate of soda together, then stir the mixture into the syrup mixture along with the beaten eggs and the milk.
5 Spread half the mixture in the prepared tin, then add the coconut mixture. Spread the remaining cake mixture in the tin and level the top. Bake in the centre of the oven for 45 to 50 minutes until firm to the touch. Allow the cake to cool in the tin for 10 minutes, then turn it out on to a wire rack, peel off the lining paper and leave to cool completely.
6 To make the topping, put the coconut milk powder and sifted icing sugar into a bowl and stir together. Stir in the water to give a smooth consistency. Pour over the cake.
7 Put the reserved coconut icing into a saucepan over a medium heat and heat for a few minutes until it turns golden brown; be careful it does not catch and burn. Sprinkle this over the top of the cake.

Cooks' Tip
Instant coconut milk powder gives the icing a rich flavour. If you can't find it, dissolve a little creamed coconut (available in blocks) in boiling water and add to the icing sugar.

Fresh cakes

Here's a selection of great-tasting cakes that are certain to become firm favourites with your family and friends. You'll find ideas for using seasonal fruits, when they are most flavourful and cheapest, as well as more unusual cake ingredients, such as carrots, courgettes, and even fresh lavender. I'm sure you'll never be at a loss for what to bake again.

RHUBARB AND GINGER STREUSAL

Time to make: 25 minutes
Time to bake: 1¼ hours
Makes a 20 cm (8 in) round cake that cuts into 10 slices

375 g (12 oz) rhubarb
30 g (1 oz) stem ginger, well drained
185 g (6 oz) butter, at room temperature
185 g (6 oz) sugar
3 eggs, size 3, lightly beaten, and at room temperature
185 g (6 oz) self-raising flour

Topping

125 g (4 oz) plain flour
60 g (2 oz) butter
90 g (3 oz) demerara sugar
1 teaspoon ground ginger

Storing and Freezing

Store for up to 4 days in a cake tin.
Freeze for up to 1 month in a plastic bag or in an airtight container. Defrost for 5 to 6 hours at room temperature.

A moist, fruity cake that I like to make when I have a garden glut or have been to a pick-your-own fruit farm and come back with too much fruit. I think this is particularly good served warm with Greek-style yogurt, and sometimes I serve it as a pudding with custard. You can also use other fruits such as blackberries, plums, gooseberries or raspberries, and add cinnamon instead of the ginger.

1 Set the oven to 180C, 350F, Gas 4. Grease a 20 cm (8 in) round deep cake or springform tin and line the base with greaseproof paper. Slice the rhubarb thickly and set aside. Chop the ginger and set aside.
2 Put the butter and sugar into a large bowl and cream together until light and fluffy. Gradually beat in the eggs, adding a little of the flour if the mixture begins to curdle. Fold in the remaining flour, along with the ginger.
3 Spread the mixture in the prepared tin and level the top. Scatter the rhubarb over the top.
4 To make the topping, rub the plain flour, butter and demerara sugar together, then stir in the ground ginger. Sprinkle the topping over the rhubarb.
5 Bake the cake in the centre of the oven for about 1¼ hours until firm to the touch. Allow the cake to cool in the tin for 10 minutes, then turn it out on to a wire rack, peel off the lining paper and leave to cool completely.

Sprinkling the topping over the rhubarb.

DONDI'S ORANGE CAKE

Time to make: 25 minutes
Time to bake: 55 minutes to 1 hour
Makes a 25 × 18 cm (10 × 7 in) cake that cuts into 12 squares

4 unwaxed oranges
125 g (4 oz) butter, at room temperature
125 g (4 oz) soft margarine
315 g (10 oz) granulated sugar
2 eggs, size 3, lightly beaten
440 g (14 oz) self-raising flour

Icing

6 tablespoons icing sugar
3 tablespoons fresh orange juice

Storing and Freezing
Store for up to 2 weeks in a cake tin.
Freeze whole or sliced for up to 1 month in a plastic bag or an airtight container. Defrost the whole cake for 5 to 6 hours at room temperature or slices for 2 to 3 hours at room temperature.

This moist cake was developed by Jacqui Hine, who worked on *Family Circle* many years ago. I believe the original recipe was given to her by the owner of her local Italian delicatessen, and it has remained a favourite of mine for many years. Fresh orange juice helps give this cake its light texture and golden colour. You can, of course, use juice from a carton, but I like the extra flavour of the freshly grated rind that you get from using fresh oranges. The icing is only a thin glaze so it is not too sweet.

1 Set the oven to 180C, 350F, Gas 4. Grease a 25 × 18 cm (10 × 7 in) base measurement roasting tin and line the base with greaseproof paper. Grate the orange rind and squeeze the juice; you will need 315 ml (10 fl oz). Set aside.
2 Place the butter and margarine into a saucepan over a low heat until just melted, then remove the pan from the heat.
3 Add the grated orange rind and juice and the sugar to the pan and stir together well. Add the eggs to the pan with the flour and beat until well blended and smooth.
4 Spread the mixture in the prepared tin and level the top. Bake in the centre of the oven for 55 minutes to 1 hour until firm to the touch and a skewer inserted into the centre comes out clean.
5 Meanwhile, to make the icing, sift the icing sugar into a small bowl, then gradually stir in the orange juice to make a thin glaze. Pour it over the hot cake and leave the cake to cool in the tin on a wire rack.
6 When the cake is completely cool, turn it out of the tin and peel off the lining paper.

Cook's Tip
If you want to eat the cake within a few days, use 315 ml (10 fl oz) vegetable oil instead of the butter and margarine, but if you want to keep the cake longer the butter and margarine will develop a better flavour.

FRESH LEMON CAKE

Time to make: 35 minutes
Time to bake: 1 hour
Makes a 20 cm (8 in) round cake that cuts into 10 to 12 slices

3 unwaxed lemons

185 g (6 oz) sunflower margarine

220 g (7 oz) caster sugar

3 eggs, size 3, lightly beaten and at room temperature

280 g (9 oz) self-raising flour

90 ml (3 fl oz) milk

Icing

155 g (5 oz) icing sugar

½ unwaxed lemon

2 tablespoons lemon curd

Storing and Freezing
Store for up to 1 week in a cake tin.
Open freeze until icing is firm, then place in a plastic bag or an airtight container and freeze for up to 1 month. Defrost for 5 to 6 hours at room temperature.

With its fresh sharp flavour, this is one of my favourite cakes. It is a variation on a traditional Greek cake where just a lemon juice and sugar syrup is poured over the warm cake and left to soak in to give a strong citrus flavour. I've topped my version with a glacé icing and lemon curd to make it even nicer.

1 Set the oven to 150C, 300F, Gas 2. Grease a 20 cm (8 in) round deep cake tin and line the base with greaseproof paper. Finely grate the lemon rinds and squeeze the juice and set aside separately.
2 Put the margarine and 185 g (6 oz) of the sugar in a large bowl and beat together until light and fluffy. Gradually beat in the eggs, adding a little of the flour if the mixture begins to curdle. Sift over the remaining flour and fold it in along with the lemon rind. Gently fold in the milk until the mixture forms a soft dropping consistency.
4 Spread the mixture in the prepared tin and level the top, then make a slight dent in the centre with the back of the spoon. Bake in the centre of the oven for 1 hour or until golden brown and firm to the touch.
5 When the cake comes out of the oven, put the remaining sugar into a bowl, then stir in all but 2 tablespoons of the reserved lemon juice, stirring until the sugar dissolves. Prick the warm cake all over with a cocktail stick, then pour over the lemon glaze. Allow the cake to cool completely in the tin still on the wire rack, then turn it out and peel off the lining paper.
6 To make the icing, sift the icing sugar into a small bowl, then stir in enough of the reserved lemon juice to make a spreadable icing. Spoon the icing on top of the cake. Put the lemon curd into a small saucepan over a low heat and warm slightly until it starts to melt. (Or, heat on High in a microwave for 20 seconds.)
7 Drizzle over the icing. Draw lines across the icing with a cocktail stick to give a featured effect.

Photographed on page 47

MARMALADE RIPPLE RING

Time to make: 20 minutes
Time to bake: 40 to 45 minutes
Makes a ring cake that cuts into 8 slices

3 unwaxed oranges

4 tablespoons orange marmalade

185 g (6 oz) sunflower margarine, at room temperature

185 g (6 oz) caster sugar

3 eggs, size 3, lightly beaten and at room temperature

250 g (8 oz) self-raising flour

Storing and Freezing
Store for up to 5 days in a cake tin.
Freeze for up to 2 months in a plastic bag or an airtight container. Defrost for 3 to 4 hours at room temperature.

Marmalade Ripple Ring (back) with Fresh Lemon Cake, *see page 45*

London chef Gary Rhodes inspired this cake when he served the most amazing marmalade steamed pudding with marmalade ice cream at The Scottish Food Proms in Glasgow. As soon as I got home, I decided I had to have a go at making a marmalade cake, and this is the result. I won't even pretend that this cake is as good as his pudding – but it does have a wonderful orange flavour. Use a strong marmalade for the best result. I like this served with custard as a dessert, too, or better still, serve it with a marmalade ice cream.

1 Set the oven to 160C, 325F, Gas 3. Thickly butter and flour a 1.25 litre (2½ pint) ring tin, tapping out any excess flour.
2 To make the topping, grate the rind from 2 of the oranges and set aside. Using a sharp knife, cut off all the white pith from both oranges, then cut each into slices. Arrange the slices in the bottom of the ring tin.
3 To make the ripple mixture, grate the rind and squeeze the juice from the remaining orange. Warm 3 tablespoons of the marmalade in a small saucepan over a medium heat. (Or, heat on High in the microwave for 30 seconds.) Stir in the orange rind from all 3 oranges.
4 Place the margarine, sugar, eggs, flour and 2 tablespoons of orange juice into a large bowl and mix with a wooden spoon for 2 to 3 minutes until smooth and well blended. Add the marmalade and orange rind and gently swirl it through the cake mixture. Do not over-mix or you will not get a rippled effect.
5 Spread the cake mixture into the prepared tin and level the top. Bake in the centre of the oven for 40 to 45 minutes or until firm to the touch. Allow the cake to cool in the tin until almost completely cool, then turn it out on to a wire rack or plate.
6 Warm the remaining tablespoon of marmalade and brush or spoon it over the orange slices to give a glaze.

DEVON APPLE CAKE

Time to make: 30 minutes
Time to bake: 1 hour
Makes a 20 cm (8 in) square cake that cuts into 10 slices, or a 23 cm (9 in) round cake that cuts into 10 slices

500 g (1 lb) cooking apples
185 g (6 oz) butter or block margarine, at room temperature
185 g (6 oz) caster sugar
3 eggs, size 3, lightly beaten and at room temperature
375 g (12 oz) self-raising flour
250 g (8 oz) mixed dried fruit
1 tablespoon mixed spice
about 3 tablespoons milk
icing sugar, for dusting

Storing and Freezing
Store for up to 4 days in a cake tin.
Freeze slices for up to 3 months in a plastic bag or an airtight container. Defrost each slice in the microwave on High for 30 seconds or for about 10 minutes in the oven at 180C, 350F, Gas 4.

This recipe is made by my mother in huge quantities every autumn when the windfall apples drop. I don't know why this recipe is particular to Devon, but having been brought up there, where our family and friends and all the tea shops each had their own particular recipe, this certainly reminds me of home. I guess the identification with Devon is because there are so many apple orchards there and also because the cake is so delicious served warm with clotted cream. It freezes well and makes an ideal moist cake for lunch boxes and picnics.

1 Set the oven to 180C, 350F, Gas 4. Grease a 20 cm (8 in) square cake tin or a 23 cm (9 in) round cake tin and line the base with greaseproof paper. Peel, core and roughly chop the apples.
2 Put the butter or margarine and sugar into a bowl and cream together until light and fluffy. Gradually beat in the eggs, adding a little of the flour if the mixture starts to curdle, then fold in the remaining flour with the fruit and spice. Stir in the apples with enough milk to give a soft dropping consistency.
3 Spread the mixture in the prepared tin and level the top. Bake in the centre of the oven for about 1 hour or until firm to the touch. Allow the cake to cool in the tin for 10 minutes, then turn out on to a wire rack, peel off the lining paper and leave to cool completely. Serve warm or leave to cool completely. To serve, dust with icing sugar.

PASSION FRUIT ANGEL CAKE

Time to make: 30 minutes
Time to bake: 45 to 50 minutes
Makes an 20 cm (8 in) ring cake that cuts into 8 to 10 slices

2 teaspoons cream of tartar
155 g (5 oz) caster sugar
90 g (3 oz) plain flour
7 egg whites, size 3, at room temperature
½ teaspoon vanilla essence

Decoration

2 tiny pink rose buds
1 egg white, size 3
caster sugar

Filling and Topping

470 ml (15 fl oz) double cream
2 tablespoons apricot jam
2 passion fruit

Storing and Freezing
Store for up to 3 days in the fridge.
Freeze for up to 1 month without the cream filling in a plastic bag or an airtight container. Defrost for 3 to 4 hours at room temperature, then fill and ice.

I'm very fond of this fluffy white cake made from egg whites. It is very light and ideal for a summer alfresco lunch or tea party. But because the cake itself is quite sweet, I think it's a good idea to fill it with sharp fresh fruits such as passion fruit and fresh cream. Alpine strawberries and oranges or fresh raspberries are equally delicious.

1 Set the oven to 160C, 325F, Gas 3. Thickly butter a 1.25 litre (2½ pint) ring tin. Dust with flour, tapping out any excess.
2 Sift the cream of tartar, sugar and flour together twice. Put the egg whites into a clean grease-free bowl and whisk until they form stiff peaks. Use a large metal spoon to fold the sifted sugar and flour and the vanilla essence into the egg whites.
3 Spread the mixture into the prepared tin and level the top. Bake in the centre of the oven for 45 to 50 minutes until the cake is springy but firm to the touch. Remove from the oven and run a round-bladed knife round the inside edge while the cake is still warm to help loosen it from the tin.
4 Invert the tin on to a wire rack and allow the cake to cool completely. When cool, remove the tin.
5 Meanwhile, to make the decoration, remove the rose petals from the buds. Put the egg white into a small bowl and beat with a fork. Use a small paintbrush to brush the flower petals very lightly with a little egg white, then sprinkle them with caster sugar. Leave the flowers to dry in a warm place for at least 1 hour before placing them on the cake.
6 To make the filling and topping, put the cream into a bowl and whip until it just holds its shape. Stir the jam into the cream. Cut the passion fruit in half and scoop the seeds into a sieve. Press the juice into the bowl of cream and stir in.
7 Use a long serrated knife to cut the cake in half horizontally, then use half the cream to sandwich the halves together. Spread the remaining cream over the top and sides of cake. Just before serving, add the crystallised rose petals.

RASPBERRY AND WHITE CHOCOLATE CAKE

Time to make: 30 minutes
Time to bake: 1¼ to 1½ hours
Makes a 20 cm (8 in) round cake that cuts into 10 slices

125 g (4 oz) white chocolate
250 g (8 oz) self-raising flour
large pinch of salt
185 g (6 oz) butter
60 g (2 oz) ground almonds
125 g (4 oz) caster sugar
2 eggs, size 3, lightly beaten and at room temperature
4 tablespoons milk
1 teaspoon vanilla essence
375 g (12 oz) fresh or frozen (but not thawed) raspberries
icing sugar, to dust

Topping

155 g (5 oz) vanilla-flavoured fromage frais
125 g (4 oz) fresh or frozen raspberries
white chocolate curls, see page 36

Storing and Freezing
Store the cake without any topping for up to 2 days in a cake tin, but with fromage frais store for 1 day only in the fridge.

Freeze without the topping for up to 1 month in a plastic bag or an airtight container. Defrost for 5 to 6 hours at room temperature, then top.

Raspberry and White Chocolate Cake

This is a very moist cake to serve for afternoon tea when friends call around, or for a summer buffet party. It certainly went down a treat at an open-air music concert I took it to! If you simply dust it with icing sugar it will keep for a day or two, but when it is topped with fromage frais it needs to be kept in the fridge and eaten quickly.

1 Set the oven to 180C, 350F, Gas 4. Grease a 20 cm (8 in) round deep or springform cake tin and line the base with greaseproof paper. Roughly chop the white chocolate; set aside.
2 Sift the flour and salt into a large bowl. Rub in the butter until the mixture resembles breadcrumbs, then stir in the ground almonds and sugar.
3 Beat the eggs, milk and vanilla essence together, then beat into the flour mixture until well blended and smooth. Stir in the chocolate and raspberries; do not over-beat or you will break up the fruit.
4 Spoon the mixture into the prepared tin and level the top. Bake in the centre of the oven for 1¼ to 1½ hours until firm to the touch. Allow the cake to cool in the tin for 10 minutes, then turn it out on to a wire rack, peel off the lining paper and leave to cool completely.
5 When the cake is completely cool, spoon the fromage frais over the top and scatter with raspberries. Decorate with chocolate curls.

Variation
I have also made this using a mixture of frozen summer fruits including strawberries, raspberries, redcurrants and cherries, and the results were just as delicious.

CARROT CAKE

Time to make: 40 minutes
Time to bake: 1 hour to 70 minutes
Makes a 20 cm (8 in) round cake that cuts into 12 slices

185 g (6 oz) carrots
1 large orange
125 g (4 oz) walnut pieces
220 ml (7 fl oz) sunflower oil
4 eggs, size 3, at room temperature
185 g (6 oz) self-raising wholemeal flour
185 g (6 oz) self-raising flour
185 g (6 oz) light muscovado sugar
1 teaspoon grated nutmeg
1 teaspoon ground cinnamon

Cream Cheese Frosting

90 g (3 oz) butter, softened
90 g (3 oz) full-fat soft cheese
drop of vanilla essence
125 g (4 oz) icing sugar

Decorations (optional)

125 g (4 oz) almond paste
green and orange food colourings (optional)

Storing and Freezing
Store for up to 1 week in cake tin.
Open freeze the cake until the frosting is firm, then freeze for up to 1 month in a plastic bag or in an airtight container. Defrost for 8 hours in the fridge.

My close friend and the commissioning editor of this book, Gill MacLennan, gave me this recipe. She used to sell the cakes to a local wholefood shop. Their customers couldn't get enough of it, and I agree it is the best carrot cake ever! This cake is also called Passion Cake.

1 Set the oven to 150C, 300F, Gas 2. Grease a 20 cm (8 in) round deep cake tin and line the base with greaseproof paper. Coarsely grate the carrots and set aside. Grate the orange rind and squeeze the juice and set aside. Roughly chop the walnuts and set aside.
2 Measure the oil into a large measuring jug, then add the eggs and lightly whisk together.
3 Place both flours, the sugar, nutmeg and cinnamon into a large mixing bowl. Add the carrots, orange rind and juice, walnuts and oil and egg mixture and beat with a wooden spoon for 1 to 2 minutes until well blended.
5 Pour the mixture into the prepared tin and level the top. Bake in the centre of the oven for 1 hour to 70 minutes until firm to the touch. Allow the cake to cool in the tin for 10 minutes, then turn it out on to a wire rack, peel off the lining paper and leave to cool completely.
6 Meanwhile, make the cream cheese frosting. Put the butter, soft cheese and vanilla into a bowl and beat until well blended and smooth. Sift in the icing sugar and beat again until smooth.
7 Spread the frosting over the top and sides of the cool cake.
8 If you like, you can make decorations for the top of the cake. Colour most of the almond paste orange, then shape into tiny carrots. Colour a little almond paste green and shape into the carrots' fronds. Arrange on top of cake.

Photographed on page 55

COURGETTE CAKE

Time to make: 25 minutes
Time to bake: 80 minutes
Makes a 20 cm (8 in) round cake that cuts into 10 slices

220 g (7 oz) walnuts or pecans
500 g (1 lb) courgettes
185 ml (6 fl oz) sunflower oil
375 g (12 oz) caster sugar
3 eggs, size 3
315 g (10 oz) plain flour
1½ teaspoons baking powder
1 teaspoon bicarbonate of soda
1½ teaspoons ground cinnamon
1 teaspoon grated nutmeg
1 teaspoon salt
125 g (4 oz) sultanas

Orange Cheese Frosting

1 unwaxed orange
125 g (4 oz) full-fat soft cheese
2 tablespoons icing sugar

Storing and Freezing
Store for up to 5 days in a cake tin. Freeze for up to 1 month in a plastic bag or an airtight container. Defrost for 8 hours at room temperature.

You may expect that this will be savoury, but it is, in fact, sweet and rather moist, like a carrot cake. It is very much the kind of cake you see in health food stores and not to everyone's taste but I like it very much. Lydia, my tester, commented that it smelt very courgettey while baking and thought it needed an icing, which I have since added. This is a great way to use up a glut of home-grown courgettes.

1 Set the oven to 180C, 350F, Gas 4. Grease a 20 cm (8 in) round deep cake tin and line the base with greaseproof paper. Finely chop the walnuts or pecans and set aside.
2 Trim the ends off the courgettes, then grate them into a large mixing bowl. Add the oil, sugar and eggs and beat together. Sift the flour, baking powder, bicarbonate of soda, cinnamon, nutmeg and salt over the courgette mixture, then fold in with 185 g (6 oz) of the walnuts or pecans and the sultanas.
3 Spoon the mixture in the prepared tin and level the top. Bake in the centre of the oven for 70 minutes or until a skewer inserted in the centre comes out clean and the cake feels firm to the touch. Allow the cake to cool in the tin for 15 minutes, then turn it out on to a wire rack, peel off the lining paper and leave to cool.
4 To make the orange cheese frosting, finely grate the orange rind into a bowl and squeeze in the juice. Add the sifted icing sugar and cheese to the orange rind with 1 tablespoon orange juice, then beat with a wooden spoon until well blended and smooth. Spread on top of the cake and sprinkle with the remaining walnuts or pecans.

Cook's Tips
I found that this quantity of mixture fitted my 1 kg (2 lb) loaf tin, but not my tester's, so I changed it to a round tin but if you prefer you can bake it in a loaf tin. If you have just a spoonful or two extra, place it into a paper cake case and bake as a cook's treat.

If you have any walnut oil, substitute about 50 ml (2 fl oz) of it for the sunflower oil for an even nuttier flavour.

MARZIPAN EASTER CAKE

Time to make: 25 minutes, plus crystallised flowers setting
Time to bake: 50 minutes to 1 hour
Makes a 20 cm (8 in) round cake that cuts into 10 slices

315 g (10 oz) almond paste
2 unwaxed oranges
2 tablespoons milk
90 g (3 oz) caster sugar
125 g (4 oz) sunflower margarine
2 eggs, size 3, at room temperature
225 g (8 oz) self-raising flour
2 teaspoons baking powder
icing sugar, for dusting

Crystallised Flowers

a few primroses and violets
1 egg white, size 3
4 tablespoons caster sugar

Storing and Freezing
Store for up to 1 week in a cake tin.
Freeze, without the almond paste topping, for up to 1 month in a plastic bag or an airtight container. Defrost for 8 hours at room temperature, then cover and grill the top.

Marzipan Easter Cake (back) with Carrot Cake, see page 52

I usually make a cake for the Easter bank holiday and last year I decided to try something different, so I developed this. It is lovely and moist, and keeps really well. For Easter, decorate this with a marzipan lattice topping and crystallised primroses and violets but for other times of the year, just dust with icing sugar.

1 Set the oven to 180C, 350F, Gas 4. Grease a 20 cm (8 in) round deep or springform cake tin and line the base with greaseproof paper. Coarsely grate 125 g (4 oz) of the almond paste and put it into a large bowl. Grate the orange rinds and squeeze 6 tablespoons juice.
2 Add the orange rind and juice to the almond paste along with the milk, sugar, margarine, eggs, flour and baking powder. Beat with a wooden spoon for 1 to 2 minutes until smooth.
3 Spread the mixture in the prepared tin and level the top. Bake in the centre of the oven for 50 minutes to 1 hour until firm to the touch and a skewer inserted in the centre comes out clean. Allow the cake to cool for 10 minutes, then turn it out on to a wire rack, peel off the lining paper and leave to cool.
4 Meanwhile, to make the crystallised flowers, remove the stems from the flowers. Put the egg white into a small bowl and beat with a fork. Use a small paintbrush to brush the flower petals very lightly with a little egg white, then sprinkle them lightly with the caster sugar. Leave the flowers to dry in a warm place for 1 to 2 hours before placing them on the cake.
5 Preheat the grill. Roll out the remaining almond paste on a work surface dusted with icing sugar. Cut into 2.5 cm (1 in) wide strips, then weave into a lattice pattern to completely cover the top of the cool cake. Trim the edges. Carefully toast the almond paste lattice under a hot grill until just golden. Add the crystallised violets and primroses.

Cook's Tips
If you think you will be pushed for time when it comes to decorating the cake, make the crystallised flowers the day before, so they have plenty of time to set. You can make the cake a day ahead and then decorate it on the day of serving.

WENSLEYDALE APPLE CAKE

Time to make: 25 minutes
Time to bake: 1 hour
Makes an 18 cm (7 in) round cake that cuts into 8 slices

185 g (6 oz) Wensleydale cheese

375 g (12 oz) Bramley cooking apples

60 g (2 oz) caster sugar

90 g (3 oz) self-raising flour

½ teaspoon baking powder

pinch of salt

30 g (1 oz) chopped hazelnuts

60 g (2 oz) sultanas

1 egg, size 3, at room temperature

4 tablespoons sunflower oil

icing sugar, to dust

Storing and Freezing
Store for up to 1 week in a cake tin. Freeze for up to 1 month in a plastic bag or an airtight container. Defrost for 8 hours at room temperature.

Photographed on page 2

As they say in the North, apple pie without cheese is like a kiss without a squeeze, and this combination of apple, hazelnuts and cheese makes a beautifully tasty, moist cake. Colleagues and I developed this recipe for a picnic feature in *BBC Good Food*, and I think it goes well with a glass of cider, too.

1 Set the oven to 180C, 350F, Gas 4. Grease an 18 cm (7 in) round deep cake tin and line the base with greaseproof paper. Cut the cheese into thick slices and set aside. Peel, core and dice the apples.
2 Place the apples into a bowl with the sugar, flour, baking powder, salt, hazelnuts and sultanas.
3 Whisk the egg and oil together with a fork, then stir into the dry ingredients.
4 Spread half the mixture into the cake tin. Arrange the cheese slices on top, then spread over the remaining cake mixture and level the top. Bake in the centre of the oven for about 1 hour or until firm to the touch. Allow the cake to cool in the tin on a wire rack until completely cool.
5 To serve, turn out of the tin, peel off the lining paper and dust the top with icing sugar.

POPPY SEED CAKE

Time to make: 20 minutes
Time to bake: 1½ hours
Makes an 18 cm (7 in) round cake that cuts into 10 slices

90 g (3 oz) poppy seeds
185 ml (6 fl oz) milk
1 unwaxed lemon
185 g (6 oz) butter, softened
185 g (6 oz) golden caster sugar
2 eggs, size 3, separated, at room temperature
250 g (8 oz) plain flour
1 teaspoon baking powder

Filling and Topping

250 g (8 oz) low-fat soft cheese
60 g (2 oz) icing sugar

Storing and Freezing
Store for up to 1 week in cake tin.
Open freeze the cake until the icing is firm, then wrap in cling film and freeze for up to 2 months. Remove the film and defrost for 5 to 6 hours at room temperature.

Variation
Use wholemeal flour if you prefer but the colour will not be as nice.

Photographed on page 59

I fell in love with the flavour of poppy seeds on a ski-ing holiday in Austria. We enjoyed the most memorable sweet yeast dumplings filled with poppy seeds and served with a sharp lemon sauce, so as soon as I got home I combined both those flavours in this cake. If you want even more of a lemon flavour, top the cake with lemon curd. This light cake is perfect for afternoon tea.

1 Set the oven to 180C, 350F, Gas 4. Grease an 18 cm (7 in) round deep cake tin and line the base with greaseproof paper.
2 Place the poppy seeds and milk into a saucepan over a medium heat and slowly bring to the boil, then remove from the heat and set aside to cool.
3 Meanwhile, use a potato peeler to thinly pare the rind from half the lemon. Cut the rind into fine shreds and reserve for the decoration. Grate the remaining lemon rind and squeeze the juice and set aside.
4 Put the butter, sugar and grated lemon rind into a large bowl and cream together until light and fluffy. Gradually beat in the egg yolks, one at a time. Stir in the poppy seeds and milk, flour and baking powder.
5 Put the egg whites into a clean grease-free bowl and whisk until they form stiff peaks. Use a large metal spoon to fold them into the cake mixture.
6 Spread the mixture into the prepared tin and level the top. Bake in the oven for about 1½ hours until firm to the touch. Allow the cake to cool in the tin for 5 minutes, then turn it out on to a wire rack, peel off the lining paper and leave to cool.
7 To make the filling and topping, put the soft cheese and about 2 tablespoons of the reserved lemon juice into a bowl. Sift in the icing sugar, then beat together until smooth.
8 Use a long serrated knife to cut the cool cake in half horizontally. Use half the filling and topping mixture to sandwich the halves together, then spread the remaining over the top. Decorate with the reserved strips of lemon rind.

LAVENDER AND ROSE PETAL CAKE

Makes an 18 cm (7 in) round cake that cuts into 10 slices
Time to make: 25 minutes
Time to bake: 45 minutes

6 heads fresh lavender
125 g (4 oz) caster sugar
125 g (4 oz) sunflower margarine
2 eggs, size 3, at room temperature
155 g (5 oz) self-raising flour
2 tablespoons milk
lavender flowers and pink rose petals, to decorate

Icing

2 to 3 tablespoons boiling water
6 tablespoons icing sugar
½ teaspoon culinary rose-water

Storing and Freezing
Store without the flower topping for up to 5 days in a cake tin, then decorate with flowers just before serving.

Freeze without flowers for up to 1 month in a plastic bag or an airtight container. Defrost for 4 to 5 hours at room temperature, then decorate.

This is simply delicious for a light summer tea, and I think it looks so pretty and summery with lavender flowers and rose petals scattered over the icing. I've iced this cake with a glacé icing flavoured with rose-water to give it an even more fragrant flavour than the lavender imparts. You can buy culinary rose-water in Greek food shops and delicatessens.

1 Set the oven to 160C, 325F, Gas 3. Grease an 18 cm (7 in) round deep or springform cake tin and line the base with greaseproof paper.
2 Strip the flowers from the lavender, then put them into a food processor with the caster sugar and whizz together. Place into a bowl with the margarine, eggs, flour and milk and beat with a wooden spoon for 2 to 3 minutes until well blended and smooth.
3 Spread the mixture in the prepared tin and level the top. Bake in the centre of the oven for about 45 minutes until firm to the touch. Allow the cake to cool in the tin for 5 minutes, then turn it out on to a wire rack, peel off the lining paper and leave to cool completely.
4 Meanwhile, make the icing. Put 2 tablespoons boiling water into a heatproof bowl, then sift in the icing sugar and stir until it is the consistency of single cream. Add an extra tablespoon water, if necessary, then stir in the rose-water and stir until smooth.
5 Pour the icing over the top of the cool cake, allowing it to drizzle down the sides a little. Scatter lavender flowers and rose petals over the top.

Cook's Tip
Use fresh lavender flowers to perfume caster sugar, then store it for weeks in an airtight jar for use in cakes and shortbread to give a lovely old-fashioned flavour. The sugar will gradually become creamy in colour and lose its fragrance, so you don't want to keep it too long.

Lavender and Rose Petal Cake (back) with Poppy Seed Cake, *see page 57*

PLUM AND HAZELNUT UPSIDE-DOWN CAKE

Time to make: 20 minutes
Time to bake: 50 to 60 minutes
Makes a 20 cm (8 in) round cake that cuts into 8 to 10 slices

1 eating apple

125 g (4 oz) self-raising flour

185 g (6 oz) wholemeal self-raising flour

1 teaspoon ground cinnamon

125 g (4 oz) butter or sunflower margarine, at room temperature

125 g (4 oz) light muscovado sugar

125 ml (4 fl oz) milk

2 eggs, size 3, beaten

Topping

60 g (2 oz) butter

60 g (2 oz) light muscovado sugar

30 g (1 oz) shelled hazelnuts, halved

500 g (1 lb) plums, halved

Storing and Freezing
Store for 3 to 4 days in a cake tin.
Freeze for up to 1 month in a plastic bag or an airtight container. Defrost for 3 to 4 hours at room temperature.

Here's a lovely autumnal cake that's a great way to make the most of plums in season. I really like this combination of flavours, but you can use apricots, peaches or other seasonal fruit.

1 Set the oven to 160C, 325F, Gas 3. Grease and line base of a 20 cm (8 in) round deep or springform cake tin.
2 To make the topping, cut the butter into small pieces and put it in a bowl with the sugar and hazelnuts. Mix together well. Sprinkle over the base of the prepared tin, then arrange the plums on top, cut sides down.
3 Peel, core and grate the apple. Put both flours in a bowl with the cinnamon. Cut the butter into small pieces and rub it in with your fingertips until the mixture resembles fine breadcrumbs. Stir in the sugar, then lightly beat in the apple, milk and eggs.
4 Spoon the mixture over the plums and level the surface. Bake in the centre of the oven for 50 to 60 minutes until risen and firm to the touch. Leave the cake to cool in the tin for 5 minutes on a wire rack, then turn it out on to a serving plate. Serve warm for pudding or cool for tea.

APRICOT APPLE CRUMBLE SQUARES

Time to make: 30 minutes
Time to bake: 30 to 40 minutes
Makes a 28 × 18 cm (11 × 7 in) cake that cuts into 12 squares

250 g (8 oz) self-raising flour
125 g (4 oz) Granary flour
½ teaspoon baking powder
185 g (6 oz) light muscovado sugar
185 g (6 oz) sunflower margarine
1 teaspoon ground cinnamon
1 egg, size 3, at room temperature
1 tablespoon milk
1 eating apple
250 g (8 oz) ready-to-eat dried apricots
30 g (1 oz) porridge oats

Storing and Freezing
Store for 3 to 4 days in a cake tin.
Freeze slices layered between non-stick baking parchment in a plastic bag or airtight container for up to 1 month. Defrost slices for 1 to 2 hours at room temperature, or microwave on High for 20 to 30 seconds per slice.

Sandwiched with a moist apple and apricot filling, this makes a delicious lunch box cake. It is the kind of cake you might expect to find in a health food shop, and I'm sure you could adapt the filling by using dates or figs instead.

1 Set the oven to 180C, 350F, Gas 4. Grease and line a 28 × 18 cm (11 × 7 in) Swiss roll tin with greaseproof paper, see page 11.
2 Place both flours, the baking powder, sugar, margarine and cinnamon in a bowl and mix with a fork until mixture resembles breadcrumbs. Be careful to make sure that any large lumps are broken up. Place half the mixture in another bowl and set aside.
3 Add the egg and milk to one half of the cake mixture, then mix to a soft paste. Spread evenly over the tin using a spatula.
4 Peel and core the apple and place into a food processor with the apricots. Whizz together until finely chopped. Spread over the cake mixture.
5 Add the oats to the remaining crumble mixture and sprinkle on top of the apricots. Bake for 30 to 40 minutes until golden brown. Allow the cake to cool completely in the tin on a wire rack, then cut into squares in the tins.

Cook's Tip
If you prefer to use dried fruit rather than the ready-to-eat plumper variety, soak them first in a little boiling water until they are soft and juicy, but not too wet.

Dried fruit cakes

There's nothing nicer than a slice of fruit cake waiting in a tin to satisfy sweet hunger pangs. I usually make one when friends or family come to stay, so there is always a snack on hand. Most of the cakes in this chapter make a suitable alternative to the traditional Christmas cake, too.

MOIST GUINNESS CAKE

Time to make: 20 minutes
Time to bake: 2½ to 3 hours
Makes a 23 cm (9 in) square cake that cuts into 14 slices

1 unwaxed orange
1 unwaxed lemon
185 g (6 oz) natural-coloured glacé cherries
375 g (12 oz) butter or margarine, at room temperature
375 g (12 oz) light muscovado sugar
6 eggs, size 3, lightly beaten and at room temperature
470 g (15 oz) plain flour
1½ teaspoons mixed spice
375 g (12 oz) raisins
280 g (9 oz) sultanas
90 g (3 oz) mixed chopped peel
185 g (6 oz) walnut pieces
235 ml (7½ fl oz) Guinness

Storing and Freezing
Store for up to 2 months re-wrapped in greaseproof paper in a cake tin.
Freeze for up to 3 months in a plastic bag or an airtight container. Defrost for 8 hours at room temperature.

Without out a doubt, one of the nicest fruit cakes I've ever made. If you can resist not tasting this cake immediately, it is best left for three to four weeks before eating to allow the flavour to mature. But this is easier said than done – I suggest you put it into a box with a 'hands off' sign on it.

1 Set the oven to 160C, 325F, Gas 3. Grease and line the base and sides of a 23 cm (9 in) square cake tin with a double layer of greaseproof paper, see page 11. Finely grate the orange and lemon rinds and set aside. Quarter the cherries and set aside.
2 Put the butter and sugar into a bowl and cream together until light and fluffy. Gradually beat in the eggs, adding a little of the flour if the mixture begins to curdle. Sift over half the flour and the mixed spice and use a large metal spoon to fold it in, then fold in all the fruit and nuts and the remaining sifted flour. Stir in the orange and lemon rinds and only half the Guinness.
3 Spread the mixture in the prepared tin and level the top. Bake in the centre of the oven for 1 hour, then reduce the oven temperature to 150C, 300F, Gas 2 and bake for a further 1½ to 2 hours or until firm to the touch. Allow the cake to cool completely in the tin on a wire rack.
4 Peel off the lining paper and prick the cool cake all over with a cocktail stick and pour over the remaining Guinness.

Spooning over the Guinness.

DUNDEE CAKE

Time to make: 20 minutes
Time to bake: 2½ to 3 hours
Makes a 20 cm (8 in) round cake that cuts into 10 slices

125 g (4 oz) candied lemon, orange and citrus peels
125 g (4 oz) currants
125 g (4 oz) raisins
125 g (4 oz) sultanas
60 g (2 oz) whole shelled almonds
1 unwaxed lemon
1 unwaxed orange
155 g (5 oz) plain flour
155 g (5 oz) plain wholemeal flour
250 g (8 oz) butter, at room temperature
250 g (8 oz) light muscovado sugar
4 eggs, size 2, lightly beaten and at room temperature
1 to 2 tablespoons milk, optional

Storing and Freezing
Store for up to 1 month in a cake tin. Freeze for up to 1 month in a plastic bag or an airtight container. Defrost for 8 hours at room temperature.

You can't beat this recipe for a traditional Scottish fruit cake with its distinctive nut topping that keeps well and is always a firm favourite. I make this when the in-laws come to stay for a week, so there is always something to dip in to the cake tin whenever anyone feels peckish. For the best, freshest flavour, I prefer to buy whole pieces of candied peel and chop it myself, rather than using the pre-diced peel that comes in tubs. If you prefer, use glacé cherries instead.

1 Set the oven to 160C, 325F, Gas 3. Grease a 20 cm (8 in) round deep cake tin and line the base and side with a double layer of greaseproof paper, see page 11. Finely chop the candied peel and put it into a large bowl.
2 Add the currants, raisins and sultanas to the chopped peel. Finely chop half the almonds, reserving the remainder for the topping, then add the chopped nuts to the bowl. Grate the lemon and orange rinds into the bowl. Sift in both flours together, adding any bran left in the sieve.
3 Put the butter and sugar in another bowl and cream together until pale and fluffy, the gradually gradually beat in the eggs, adding a little of the flour if the mixture begins to curdle. Fold in the fruit and flour mixture and add the milk, if necessary, to give a soft dropping consistency.
4 Spread the mixture in prepared cake tin, level the top and arrange the remaining almonds in a circular pattern on top. Bake in the centre of the oven for 2½ to 3 hours until firm to the touch and a skewer inserted in the centre comes out clean. Allow the cake to cool in the tin for 10 minutes, then turn it out on to a wire rack, peel off the lining paper and leave to cool completely.

SIMNEL CAKE

Time to make: 30 minutes
Time to bake: 3 hours
Makes a 20 cm (8 in) round cake that cuts into 12 to 16 slices

250 g (8 oz) plain flour
pinch of salt
1 teaspoon grated nutmeg
1 teaspoon ground cinnamon
1 unwaxed lemon
60 g (2 oz) glacé cherries
60 g (2 oz) chopped dried peel
185 g (6 oz) sultanas
185 g (6 oz) raisins
125 g (4 oz) currants
185 g (6 oz) butter, softened
185 g (6 oz) golden caster sugar
3 eggs, size 3, lightly beaten and at room temperature
2 tablespoons milk, optional
icing sugar, for dusting
500 g (1 lb) almond paste

Decorations

1 tablespoon apricot jam
125 g (4 oz) almond paste
yellow and green concentrated food colourings

Storing and Freezing

Store for up to 1 month in a cake tin.

Freeze for up to 3 months in a plastic bag or an airtight container. Defrost overnight at room temperature.

This is the traditional Simnel cake recipe served at Easter. You will usually see it decorated with eleven lightly grilled balls of almond paste to represent the eleven faithful disciples, but I prefer a prettier cake decorated with almond paste flowers.

1 Set the oven to 150C, 300F, Gas 2. Grease a 20 cm (8 in) round deep cake tin and line the base and sides with a double thickness of greaseproof paper, see page 11.

2 Sift the flour, salt, nutmeg and cinnamon into a bowl. Finely grate in the lemon rind. Cut the cherries in half, then add them to the bowl with the peel, sultanas, raisins and currants.

3 Put the butter and sugar into a large bowl and cream together until light and fluffy. Gradually beat in the eggs, adding a little of the flour if the mixture begins to curdle. Stir in the fruit and remaining flour and mix well, adding the milk if necessary to give a soft dropping consistency.

4 Dust the work surface with icing sugar. Roll out half the almond paste into a circle about 19 cm (7½ in) round. Spread half the mixture into the prepared tin and place the almond paste on top, then top with the remaining cake mixture and level the top. Bake in the centre of the oven for about 3 hours or until golden and firm. Leave to cool in the tin on a wire rack.

5 Dust the work surface with icing sugar. Roll out the remaining almond paste into a 20 cm (8 in) diameter circle. Brush the top of the cool cake with apricot jam, then place the almond paste on top. Crimp the edge between 2 fingers and your thumb.

6 To make the decorations, knead a little yellow colouring into 100 g (3½ oz) almond paste. Roll this into 25 to 30 little balls and flatten each to make a petal. Arrange 5 petals overlapping in a circle to make a flower. Make 5 or 6 flowers, then place them in the centre of the cake. Colour the remaining almond paste green. Roll out small balls and place one in the centre of each flower, then roll out small oval shaped leaves. Mark veins with the back of a knife and arrange with the flowers. Tie yellow and green ribbons together, if you like, to decorate the sides.

TREASURE ISLAND CAKE

Time to make: 40 minutes
Time to bake: 2¼ to 2½ hours
Makes a 20 cm (8 in) round cake that cuts into 14 slices

125 g (4 oz) ready-to-eat dried apricots

125 g (4 oz) natural-coloured glacé cherries

125 g (4 oz) walnuts

125 g (4 oz) almond paste

2 large unwaxed oranges

185 g (6 oz) butter, at room temperature

185 g (6 oz) golden caster sugar

3 eggs, size 3, lightly beaten and at room temperature

250 g (8 oz) sultanas

250 g (8 oz) plain wholemeal flour

1 teaspoon baking powder

2 teaspoons ground cinnamon

2 tablespoons demerara sugar, for the topping

Storing and Freezing
Store for up to 2 weeks in a cake tin. Freeze for up to 1 month in a plastic bag or an airtight container. Defrost for 8 hours at room temperature.

Treasure Island Cake with almond paste decoration (see Cook's Tip).

This is one of my most favourite and trusted recipes which I make almost every year as an alternative Christmas cake...it's moist, crumbly and contains hidden nuggets of marzipan. But it's too good to keep for just special occasions, and once you've tried it, I'm sure it will become favourite with your family, too.

1 Set the oven to 160C, 325F, Gas 3. Grease a 20 cm (8 in) round deep cake tin and line the base and sides with a double layer of greaseproof paper, see page 11. Quarter the apricots, halve the cherries and chop the walnuts, then set them aside. Roll the almond paste into marble-size balls, then set aside. Grate the rind from the oranges and squeeze about 155 ml (5 fl oz) of the juice and set aside.
2 Put the butter and sugar into a bowl and cream together until light and fluffy. Gradually beat in the eggs, adding a little of the flour if the mixture begins to curdle.
3 Add the almond paste balls, the apricots, cherries, walnuts, sultanas, orange rind and juice. Sift the flour, baking powder and cinnamon into the bowl, adding any bran remaining in the sieve. Stir together until everything is well blended.
4 Spread the mixture in the prepared tin and level the top. Place the tin on a baking sheet and bake in the centre of the oven for 1 hour. Reduce the heat to 150C, 300F, Gas 2 and bake for a further 45 minutes, then sprinkle the top with the demerara sugar. Continue baking for 30 to 45 minutes until firm to the touch, starting to shrink away from the sides of the tin and a skewer inserted into the centre comes out clean.
5 Allow the cake to cool for 10 minutes in the tin, then turn it out on to a wire rack, peel off the lining paper and leave to cool completely.

Cook's Tip
If you like, decorate with almond paste, cut into leaf shapes and arranged on top and lightly grilled, or with glacé fruit and nuts, glazed with warmed sieved apricot jam.

MUSCATEL BREAKFAST CAKE

Time to make: 15 minutes, plus 2 hours soaking
Time to bake: 1½ hours
Makes a 22 cm (8½ in) round cake that cuts into 10 slices

125 g (4 oz) walnut pieces
250 g (8 oz) raisin bran flake breakfast cereal
250 g (8 oz) Muscatel raisins
250 g (8 oz) light muscovado sugar
2 teaspoons vanilla essence
470 ml (15 fl oz) milk
250 g (8 oz) plain flour
1 tablespoon baking powder

Storing and Freezing
Store for up to 2 weeks in a cake tin. Freeze for up to 1 month in a plastic bag or an airtight container. Defrost for 8 hours at room temperature.

I first tasted this recipe many years ago when I was served it by Michael Smith, now sadly dead. He was a very generous cook who loved and promoted English food with a passion, and he liked making cakes as much as I do. I've adapted his recipe slightly and hope he would approve.

I think you'll find this dense rich cake makes a delicious rushed breakfast with a cup of coffee. It's also a natural for packing in lunch boxes. It would not be nearly as nice without the flavour of the giant sweet Muscatel raisins, and the bran flakes provide a delicious nutty flavour, as well as keeping quality.

1 Chop the walnuts, then place them into a large bowl with the breakfast cereal, raisins, sugar, vanilla and milk. Leave to soak for 2 hours or until most of the milk has been absorbed.
2 When ready to bake, set the oven to 180C, 350F, Gas 4. Grease a 22 cm (8½ in) round deep cake tin and line the base with greaseproof paper.
3 Sift the flour and baking powder on top of the bran mixture, then stir in until well blended.
4 Spread the mixture in the prepared tin and level the top. Bake in the centre of the oven for 1½ hours or until firm to the touch, covering the top with foil or greaseproof if it begins to brown too much. Turn out the cake on to a wire rack, peel off the lining paper and leave to cool completely.

CHEWY FRUIT AND OAT BARS

Time to make: 30 minutes
Time to cook: 40 minutes
Makes a 28 × 18 cm (11 × 7 in) cake that cuts into 12 slices

250 g (8 oz) eating apples
5 tablespoons orange juice
125 g (4 oz) ready-to-eat dried apricots, chopped
125 g (4 oz) sultanas
125 g (4 oz) chopped mixed nuts
90 g (3 oz) rolled oats
90 g (3 oz) self-raising wholemeal flour
60 g (2 oz) desiccated coconut
60 g (2 oz) sunflower seeds
2 tablespoons sesame seeds
2 tablespoons honey

Topping (optional)
2 tablespoons honey

Storing and Freezing
Store for up to 2 weeks in a cake tin.
Freeze for up to 1 month in an airtight container or plastic bag. Defrost for 1 hour at room temperature.

A favourite snack of mine, these are more filling, tastier and more nutritious than any cereal bar you can buy, and once made will keep for up to two weeks in a cake tin. I often take a slice to work with me for a healthy munch break.

1 Set the oven to 180C, 350F, Gas 4. Grease and line the base of a 28 × 18 cm (11 × 7 in) Swiss roll tin with greaseproof paper, see page 11.
2 Peel, core and chop the apples, then place them into a pan with the orange juice. Cover and simmer until the apples are just soft. This will only take a few minutes. Mash to a smooth purée.
3 Add all the remaining ingredients and stir well with a wooden spoon. Press mixture evenly into the prepared tin and level the surface. Bake in the centre of the oven for 40 minutes, until pale golden. Leave the cake to cool completely in the tin on a wire rack, then turn out and peel off the lining paper.
4 If you like, brush the top with honey to give a shine, then cut into 12 bars.

SCRUMPY FRUIT CAKE

Time to make: 30 minutes, plus 1 to 2 hours soaking the fruit
Time to bake: 1½ to 1¾ hours
Makes a 20 cm (8 in) round cake that cuts into 12 slices

250 g (8 oz) bag mixed dried fruit salad
7 tablespoons cider
185 g (6 oz) butter, softened
185 g (6 oz) light muscovado sugar
3 eggs, size 3, beaten and at room temperature
250 g (8 oz) self-raising flour
1 teaspoon baking powder
½ teaspoon ground ginger

Topping
30 g (1 oz) hazelnuts
3 pears
155 ml (5 fl oz) cider
4 tablespoons clear honey or ginger syrup
4 pieces stem ginger, drained and chopped
3 tablespoons rolled oats
3 tablespoons light demerara sugar

Storing and Freezing
Store for up to 5 days in a cake tin.
Freeze for up to 3 months in a plastic bag or an airtight container. Defrost for 5 to 6 hours at room temperature.

Scrumpy Fruit Cake

I lived in Devon until I was 18 years old and went to Birmingham to do my Home Economics diploma, so I was brought up on scrumpy, the popular local cider. For this cake I've soaked the fruit in cider to give it a lovely apple flavour. You can really taste it in the moist baked cake. I like rough dry ciders, but you may prefer to use a sweeter cider. The chewy bites of dried fruit salad and crumbly topping make a nice change to the more usual fruit cakes. The original inspiration for this cake comes from a feature I tore out of *Living* magazine many years ago.

1 Chop the dried fruit roughly using kitchen scissors, then put them into a bowl with the cider and leave to soak for 1 to 2 hours until plump and most of the liquid has been absorbed.
2 Set the oven to 180C, 350F, Gas 4. Grease a 20 cm (8 in) round deep loose-bottomed cake tin and line the base and sides with greaseproof paper (or it will be difficult to lift out).
3 Put the butter and sugar into a bowl and cream together until light and fluffy. Gradually beat in the eggs, adding a little of the flour if the mixture begins to curdle. Sift over the remaining flour, the baking powder and ginger and use a large metal spoon to fold in along with the fruit and any cider remaining in the bowl.
4 Spread the mixture in the prepared tin and level the surface. Bake in the centre of the oven for 1 to 1½ hours until firm.
5 Meanwhile, to make the topping, preheat the grill. Toast 30 g (1 oz) of the hazelnuts. Place them in a tea towel and rub well to remove the skins. Chop the hazelnuts roughly. Peel core and dice the pears. Put the cider and 2 tablespoons of the honey or ginger syrup into a saucepan over a medium heat and heat until melted, stirring occasionally. Stir in the pears and poach until the liquid evaporates. Remove from heat and pour in the remaining honey.
6 Spread the topping over the cake, then sprinkle with nuts, ginger, oats and sugar. Return to the oven for a further 25 minutes. Allow the cake to cool in the tin for 10 minutes, then turn it out on to a wire rack, peel off the lining paper and leave

CARIBBEAN RUM CAKE

Time to make: 45 minutes, plus overnight soaking
Time to bake: 2 to 2¼ hours
Makes a 20 cm (8 in) round cake that cuts into 14 slices

185 g (6 oz) ready-to-eat dried apricots
185 g (6 oz) ready-to-eat dried figs
185 g (6 oz) ready-to-eat dried dates
125 g (4 oz) Brazil nuts, shelled
90 g (3 oz) natural-coloured glacé cherries
425 g (14½ oz) can pineapple pieces in natural juices
185 g (6 oz) butter, softened
185 g (6 oz) dark muscovado sugar
185 ml (6 fl oz) dark rum
3 eggs, size 3
185 g (6 oz) self-raising flour
185 g (6 oz) plain flour

Topping

3 tablespoons apricot jam
250 g (8 oz) crystallised fruits, such as cherries, pineapple, oranges, lemons and apricots
90 g (3 oz) Brazil nuts, shelled and blanched

Storing and Freezing
Store for up to 3 weeks in a cake tin
Freeze without topping for up to 3 months. Defrost for 8 hours then decorate.

Very moist and boozy, this rum-soaked cake makes a tropical alternative to traditional Christmas cakes, and is ideal for any celebration. I like to decorate it piled high with crystallised fruits. These are quite expensive but dried ready-to-eat apricots and dates, brushed with warmed sieved apricot jam look just as effective and are more economical.

1 Chop the apricots, figs, dates and Brazil nuts, then place them into a large saucepan over a low heat with the cherries, pineapple pieces and 185 ml (6 fl oz) of juice from the can, the Brazil nuts, butter and sugar. Bring up to the simmering point and stir well until the sugar dissolves. Remove from the heat and stir in 125 ml (4 fl oz) of the rum, then leave to soak overnight.
2 When ready to bake, set the oven to 150C, 300F, Gas 2. Grease a 20 cm (8 in) round deep cake tin and line the base and sides with a double layer of greaseproof paper, see page 11.
3 Stir the mixture well, then beat in the eggs and flours, stirring until well blended.
4 Spread the mixture in the prepared tin and level the top with the back of the spoon. Bake in the centre of the oven for 2 to 2¼ hours until firm to the touch. Cool in tin on a wire rack.
5 Pierce the cool cake well with a cocktail stick, then pour over the remaining rum. Leave until the rum has soaked in before topping, which should take about 10 minutes. Place the apricot jam into a saucepan over a low heat and warm, then push through a fine sieve. Brush the jam over the top of the cake, then pile crystallised fruit and nuts on top.

Caribbean Rum Cake (back) with Mango and Lime Yogurt Cake, with Greek-style yogurt topping, see page 76

Traditional cakes

No self-respecting tea shop should be without one or two of these traditional cakes, and neither should any useful cake book! Though after I tested more than 75 cakes all my husband yearned for was a slice of Victoria Sandwich with jam and cream!

SWISS ROLL

Time to make: 20 minutes
Time to bake: 8 to 10 minutes
Makes one Swiss Roll that cuts into 8 slices

3 eggs, size 3, at room temperature

125 g (4 oz) caster sugar

125 g (4 oz) plain flour

FILLINGS

The classic filling for a plain Swiss roll is warmed raspberry jam, but you can use any flavour of jam. I think apricot is very good, too. Warm the jam slightly and spread over the cooled Swiss Roll before rolling up.

Buttercream Filling

Unroll the cool Swiss roll and fill with any flavour buttercream icing, together with a layer of jam, if liked.

Fresh Fruit and Cream Filling

Lightly whip 315 ml (10 fl oz) double cream until it just holds its shape, then sweeten with a little sifted icing sugar. Spread over the cool Swiss Roll and scatter with fresh fruit, then roll up. Pipe or swirl cream on top and decorate with fruit.

Mascarpone Filling

Beat 220 g (7 oz) mascarpone cheese with 1 tablespoon icing sugar, strong black coffee, grated chocolate or finely chopped nuts. Spread over the cool Swiss Roll, then roll up.

Storing and Freezing

Store for up to 2 days in a cake tin.
Freeze for up to 2 months in a plastic bag or an airtight container. Defrost for 2 hours at room temperature.

I love Swiss Rolls. They are so easy and quick to make, the perfect cake to rustle up for tea when you want something sweet, or to fill with fresh cream and fruit and turn into a dessert. This is my standby if friends call to ask if they can pop by.

1 Set the oven to 220C, 425F, Gas 7. Grease a 33 × 23 cm (13 × 9 in) Swiss roll tin and line the base and sides with greaseproof paper, see page 11. Grease the paper.
2 Place the eggs and sugar into a large bowl over a saucepan of gently simmering water. Use an electric hand-held whisk to whisk the mixture until it is thick enough to leave a definite trail when the whisk if lifted; this will take about 10 minutes. (Or, use an electric table-top mixer rather than heating it on the cooker.)
3 Sift over the flour and use a large metal spoon to fold it in, along with 1 tablespoon of hot water, taking care not to knock out any of the air. Spoon the mixture from the bottom of the bowl up over the top in a figure-of-eight motion. Cut through the mixture occasionally with the side of a spoon to break up any pockets of flour.
4 Pour the mixture into the prepared tin, tilting the tin slightly to spread the mixture evenly over the whole base. Bake in the centre of the oven for 8 to 10 minutes until risen and just firm.
5 Meanwhile, place a sheet of greaseproof paper larger than the tin on the work surface and sprinkle with caster sugar. Turn out the cake on to the paper and peel off the lining paper. Use a sharp knife to trim off all the crisp edges. Make a long cut half way through the cake 2.5 cm (1 in) away from one short end, then roll up with the paper inside so you can unroll it when it is cool. Cool on a wire rack with the seam at the bottom.
6 When the Swiss roll is cool, gently unroll it, remove the paper and fill with the filling of your choice. Gently roll up again, dust with icing sugar and place on a serving plate.

Opposite: Whisking the mixture until it is thick enough to leave a trail on the surface when the whisks are lifted.

MADEIRA CAKE

Time to make: 25 minutes
Time to bake: 1¼ to 1½ hours
Makes a 18 cm (7 in) round cake that cuts into 8 slices

1 unwaxed orange

185 g (6 oz) butter, at room temperature

185 g (6 oz) caster sugar

3 eggs, size 3, lightly beaten and at room temperature

155 g (5 oz) self-raising flour

125 g (4 oz) plain flour

1 thin slice citron peel, to decorate

Storing and Freezing
Store for up to 1 week in a cake tin. Freeze for up to 2 months in a plastic bag or an airtight container. Defrost for 5 to 6 hours at room temperature.

Serve this traditional plain cake with a glass of Madeira wine or just a cup of refreshing tea. For the best flavour, it is essential that you use good-quality butter, and the cake should traditionally be topped with a delicious slice of citron peel, but this is not really necessary.

I like the flavour of orange juice in this cake but I think you will still be happy with the result if you use milk and a little vanilla essence instead.

1 Set the oven to 160C, 325F, Gas 3. Grease an 18 cm (7 in) round deep cake tin and line the base with greaseproof paper. Finely grate the orange rind and squeeze the juice.
2 Put the butter and sugar into a bowl and cream together until light and fluffy. Gradually beat in the eggs, adding a little flour if it begins to curdle. Sift over the flours together, then fold them into the creamed mixture along with the orange rind and 2 tablespoons of the juice.
3 Spread the mixture in the prepared tin and level the top. Place the citron peel in the centre. Bake in the centre of the oven for about 1¼ to 1½ hours or until firm to the touch. Allow the cake to cool in the tin for 10 minutes, then turn out on to a wire rack, peel off the lining paper and leave to cool completely.

Variation
For an old-fashioned seed cake, just add 2 teaspoons caraway seeds to the mixture.

VICTORIA SANDWICH CAKE

Time to make: 15 minutes
Time to bake: 25 to 30 minutes
Makes a 15 cm (6 in) cake that cuts into 8 slices

125 g (4 oz) butter, at room temperature

125 g (4 oz) caster sugar

2 eggs, size 3, lightly beaten and at room temperature

125 g (4 oz) self-raising sponge flour

1 tablespoon milk, optional

4 tablespoons raspberry jam, for filling

caster sugar, for dusting

Storing and Freezing
Store for up to 5 days in a cake tin. Freeze for up to 1 month in a plastic bag or an airtight container. Defrost for 3 to 4 hours at room temperature.

VARIATIONS

Coffee Sponge
Add 1 tablespoon instant coffee granules dissolved in 2 teaspoons hot water to the cake mixture.

Chocolate Sponge
Replace 30 g (1 oz) of the flour with 30 g (1 oz) cocoa powder.

Cardamom Sponge
Add the finely grated rind of 1 unwaxed lemon, 1 teaspoon lemon juice and the crushed seeds of 6 cardamom pods to the creamed mixture. Fill with 3 tablespoons lemon curd and 155 ml (5 fl oz) whipped cream. Dust the top of the cake with icing sugar.

I couldn't imagine doing this book without including this English classic. This was probably the first cake I ever made as a girl, and it is still maddeningly my husband's favourite. The secret of a light cake is to cream the butter and sugar very well and add the eggs very gradually. If you start with all the ingredients at room temperature and take your time, I guarantee you'll make a prize-winning cake. This is also an extremely good base for any children's birthday or novelty cakes, filled and decorated with buttercream, see below right. For a classic Victoria Sponge, however, fill your cake with raspberry jam – and I think home-made is best.

1 Set the oven to 190C, 375F, Gas 5. Grease two 15 cm (6 in) round sandwich tins and line the bases with greaseproof paper. Flour the tins well, then tap out any excess flour.
2 Put the butter and sugar into a large bowl and cream together until pale, light and creamy; it is important to cream the mixture well at this stage to incorporate as much air in as possible and to prevent the mixture curdling when you add the eggs.
3 Gradually beat the eggs into the creamed mixture, a little at a time, until well blended and smooth; the more thoroughly and gradually you beat them in, the less likely the mixture is to curdle. If the mixture does begin to curdle, however, beat in a little of the flour.
4 Sift the remaining flour over and use a large metal spoon to fold it into the creamed mixture. Take care not to over-mix the mixture because you will knock out all the air. If the mixture feels very stiff, add 1 tablespoon milk to give a soft dropping consistency.
5 Spread the mixture evenly in the prepared tins and level the tops. Bake in the centre of the oven for 25 to 30 minutes until pale golden brown and firm to touch. Allow the cakes to cool in the tins for 5 minutes, then turn them out on to wire racks, peel off the lining papers and leave to cool completely.
6 When the cakes are cool, sandwich them together with jam and dust with caster sugar.

DATE AND WALNUT CAKE

Time to make: 25 minutes
Time to bake: 1½ hours
Make an 18 cm (7 in) cake that cuts into 8 slices

185 g (6 oz) dates, stoned
125 g (4 oz) self-raising flour
125 g (4 oz) self-raising wholemeal flour
pinch of salt
pinch of mixed spice
125 g (4 oz) block margarine or butter
90 g (3 oz) caster sugar
60 g (2 oz) walnut pieces
1 egg, size 3
about 2 tablespoons milk
60 g (2 oz) granulated sugar, for the topping

Storing and Freezing
Store for up to 2 weeks in a cake tin. Freeze for up to 3 months in a plastic bag or an airtight container. Defrost for 5 to 6 hours at room temperature.

Date and Walnut Cake (back) with Classic Gingerbread, see page 84

Here's a wonderful old-fashioned cake that never fails to please. As far back as I can remember, my mum always kept a block of cooking dates in her larder for making this cake, and I always used to sneak in a pinch a chunk. Be sure to use plump dried dates, to ensure you get lovely chewy bites. For a real treat use Medjool dates but I have to warn you they are very expensive. This is quite a plain cake so feel free to add extra dates and nuts if you want. Or, if you want a more attractive-looking cake, use a few to decorate the top, but I prefer this rustic look.

1 Set the oven to 180C, 350F, Gas 4. Grease an 18 cm (7 in) round deep cake tin and line the base with greaseproof paper. Roughly chop the dates.
2 Sift the flours together, adding any bran left in the sieve, with the salt and spice. Add the margarine or butter and rub it in with your fingertips until the mixture resembles fine breadcrumbs. Stir in the sugar, dates and walnuts.
3 Lightly beat the egg and add it with sufficient milk to give the mixture a soft dropping consistency.
4 Spread the mixture in the prepared tin and level the top. Bake in the centre of the oven for 1½ hours or until firm. Just before the end of baking time, dissolve the sugar in 2 to 3 tablespoons water into a small saucepan, then bring to the boil and boil for 2 to 3 minutes until syrupy. Brush over the top of the cake and return it to the oven to finish baking.
5 Allow the cake to cool in the tin for 10 minutes, then turn it out on to a wire rack, peel off the lining paper and allow the cake to cool completely.

CLASSIC GINGERBREAD

Time to make: 20 minutes
Time to bake: 1¼ hours
Makes a 27 × 23 cm (11 × 9 in) cake that cuts into 16 squares

500 g (1 lb) plain flour
4 teaspoons ground ginger
1 tablespoon baking powder
1 teaspoon bicarbonate of soda
1 teaspoon salt
250 g (8 oz) light or dark muscovado sugar
185 g (6 oz) margarine
375 g (12 oz) black treacle or golden syrup
315 ml (10 fl oz) milk
1 egg, size 3

Storing and Freezing
Store for up to 2 weeks in a cake tin.
Freeze slices for up to 2 months in a plastic bag or an airtight container. Defrost for 1 to 2 hours at room temperature.

I've been making this foolproof basic recipe for about as many years as I can remember. One of its great advantages is that it can easily be adapted by adding chopped stem ginger, sultanas or chopped orange peel to the mixture. Sometimes I also like to reduce the treacle or syrup by one or two tablespoonfuls and add thick-cut marmalade instead. If you can resist the temptation to eat this as soon as it cools, it really is best if it is allowed to mature for a day or two. To decorate the top, if you want, just drizzle with glacé icing and top with slices of stem ginger.

1 Set the oven to 160C, 325F, Gas 2. Grease a 27 × 23 cm (11 × 9 in) roasting tin and line the base with greaseproof paper.
2 Sift the flour, ginger, baking powder, bicarbonate of soda and salt into a large bowl. Place the sugar, margarine, treacle or syrup into a saucepan over a medium heat and heat until the butter just melts; do not allow the mixture to become too hot. Stir in the milk to help it cool a little, then beat in the egg. Pour into the dry ingredients and beat together.
3 Pour the mixture immediately in the prepared tin. Bake in the centre of the oven for about 1¼ hours until firm to the touch. Allow the gingerbread to cool in the tin for 10 minutes, then turn it out on to a wire rack, peel off the lining paper and leave to cool completely.

Cook's Tip
If you like your gingerbread really spicy, add 1 to 2 teaspoons ground ginger and some freshly ground black pepper.

Photographed on page 83

YORKSHIRE PARKIN

Time to make: 15 minutes
Time to bake: 1 hour
Makes a 20 cm (8 in) square cake that cuts into 12 squares

60 g (2 oz) stem ginger, well drained
155 ml (5 fl oz) milk
2 teaspoons bicarbonate of soda
185 g (6 oz) golden syrup
60 g (2 oz) black treacle
90 g (3 oz) light muscovado sugar
250 g (8 oz) butter or margarine
250 g (8 oz) oatmeal
250 g (8 oz) plain flour
pinch of salt
good pinch of black pepper
good pinch of ground cardamom
2 teaspoons ground ginger, or 1 tablespoon freshly grated fresh root ginger

Storing and Freezing
Store for up to 1 month in a cake tin.
Freeze squares for up to 1 month in a plastic bag or an airtight container. Defrost squares for about 30 minutes at room temperature.

This is my spicy version of traditional Yorkshire parkin, flavoured with black pepper and cardamom, but you can omit these ingredients if you prefer. I also like to use freshly grated ginger. Parkin has a chewy oatmeal texture with a lovely sticky topping. It is best left for one to two days to mature before cutting and definitely improves with keeping.

1 Set the oven to 160C, 325F, Gas 3. Grease a 20 cm (8 in) square deep cake tin and line the base with greaseproof paper. Roughly chop the ginger and set aside.
2 Measure the milk into a measuring jug, then add the bicarbonate of soda and stir to dissolve. Place the golden syrup, treacle, sugar and butter or margarine into a large saucepan over a medium heat and stir until the sugar dissolves and the butter or margarine melts.
3 Remove the pan from the heat and stir in the oatmeal, flour, salt, spices, milk and stem ginger, beating together until well blended and smooth.
4 Pour the mixture in the prepared tin. Bake in the centre of the oven for 1 hour until just firm to the touch. Allow the cake to cool completely in the tin on a wire rack; the cake will sink slightly in the centre.

Loaf cakes

Here's a selection of cut-and-come-again cakes. These are easy to slice and pack for picnics and lunch boxes and are usually very moist, as well as filled with flavour. I think you will find these are suitable for almost every occasion. Served plain, these are just the thing to enjoy with a cup of tea, but they also make a quick mid-week dessert if served with a scoop of ice cream.

PUMPKIN AND CINNAMON LOAF

Time to make: 20 minutes
Time to bake: 45 to 50 minutes
Makes a 1 kg (2 lb) loaf that cuts into 8 slices

375 g (12 oz) fresh pumpkin with the thick peel removed

185 g (6 oz) butter

155 g (5 oz) clear honey

1 egg, size 3

125 g (4 oz) light muscovado sugar

375 g (12 oz) self-raising wholemeal flour

2 teaspoons ground cinnamon

butter, at room temperature, for serving

Storing and Freezing
Store for up to 3 days in a cake tin. Freeze for up to 1 month in a plastic bag or an airtight container. Defrost for 5 to 6 hours at room temperature.

It's wonderful working at *BBC Good Food* because so often a cake arrives warm from the oven for tasting. Mary Cadogan, my deputy editor and fellow cake baker, developed this moist and spicy recipe for a pumpkin feature. It is simply delicious served buttered for tea. It is also incredibly quick and easy, and an ideal way to use up the pumpkin that you've scooped out of the children's Halloween lantern.

1 Set the oven to 180C, 350F, Gas 4. Grease a 1 kg (2 lb) loaf tin and line the base and sides with greaseproof paper, see page 11. Grate the pumpkin and set aside.
2 Place the butter into a small saucepan over a medium heat and melt it. (Or, melt in the microwave on High for 1½ minutes.)
3 Pour the butter into the bowl and add the honey and egg. Stir in the pumpkin, then add the sugar, flour and cinnamon and beat until well blended.
4 Spread the mixture in the prepared tin and level the top. Bake in the centre of the oven for 45 to 50 minutes until a skewer inserted in the centre comes out clean and the loaf is firm to the touch.
5 Allow the loaf to cool in the tin for 5 minutes, then turn it out on to a wire rack, peel off the lining paper and leave to cool completely. Serve sliced and buttered.

Stirring the pumpkin mixture.

PINEAPPLE AND SULTANA CAKE

Time to make: 20 minutes
Time to bake: 1 hour
Make a 1 kg (2 lb) loaf that cuts into 8 slices

250 g (8 oz) pineapple rings in natural juice
250 g (8 oz) self-raising flour
2 teaspoons baking powder
125 g (4 oz) demerara sugar
125 g (4 oz) sunflower margarine
2 eggs, size 3
185 g (6 oz) sultanas
60 g (2 oz) desiccated coconut

Decoration

30 g (1 oz) coconut flakes
4 tablespoons icing sugar
30 g (1 oz) crystallised pineapple

Storing and Freezing
Store for up to 2 weeks in a cake tin.
Freeze for up to 3 months in a plastic bag or an airtight container. Defrost for 8 hours at room temperature.

This is a very easy, crumbly cake made using the all-in-one method. The pineapple gives it a delicious flavour and helps to keep it moist. Make sure you use canned pineapple in natural juices not sugar syrup. If you don't like coconut, just leave it out, but personally I love this tropical combination. Look in health food shops for the large flakes of coconut for the decoration but if you don't find those use desiccated coconut.

1 Set the oven to 160C, 325F, Gas 3. Grease a 1 kg (2 lb) loaf tin and line the base and sides with greaseproof paper, see page 11. Drain and finely chop the pineapple and put into a large bowl along with 6 tablespoons of the juice. Reserve a few drops of juice for the topping and set aside.
2 Add the flour, baking powder, sugar, margarine, eggs, sultanas and coconut to the bowl and beat together for 1 to 2 minutes until well blended and smooth.
3 Spread the mixture in the prepared tin and level the top. Bake in the centre of the oven for 1 hour or until golden and firm to the touch. Allow the cake to cool in the tin for 10 minutes, then turn it out on to a wire rack, peel off the lining paper and leave to cool completely.
4 To decorate, preheat the grill. Place the coconut flakes on a baking sheet and toast until they are just golden under the grill. Sift the icing sugar into a bowl, then mix with a few drops of the reserved pineapple juice to make the consistency of single cream. Drizzle the icing over the cake. Chop the crystallised pineapple and scatter over the top with the toasted coconut.

BANANA AND DATE LOAF

Time to make: 20 minutes
Time to bake: 1 hour
Makes a 1 kg (2 lb) loaf that cuts into 10 slices

125 g (4 oz) dried pitted dates
500 g (1 lb) ripe bananas, about 3 all together
125 g (4 oz) plain flour
125 g (4 oz) plain wholemeal flour
2 teaspoons baking powder
125 g (4 oz) sunflower margarine
90 g (3 oz) light or dark muscovado sugar
2 eggs, size 3, beaten
1 tablespoon milk, optional
60 g (2 oz) sweetened dried banana chips

Storing and Freezing
Store for up to 1 week in a cake tin.
Freeze whole or sliced in a plastic bag or an airtight container for up to 3 months. Defrost the whole loaf for 5 to 6 hours at room temperature and the slices for 1 hour at room temperature.

I have been making this cake for more than fifteen years. Whenever I see slightly blackened ripe bananas that are being sold cheaply, I use them as an excuse to make this moist yummy cake. The flavour of bananas really comes through. If you prefer, omit the dates, or add chocolate chips instead.

1 Preheat the oven to 180C, 350F, Gas 4. Grease a 1 kg (2 lb) loaf tin and line the base and sides with greaseproof paper, see page 11. Finely chop the dates and set aside.
2 Peel and mash the bananas into a large bowl, then add the flours, baking powder, margarine, sugar and eggs and beat with a wooden spoon for 1 to 2 minutes until just blended and smooth. Add the milk, if necessary to give a soft dropping consistency. Stir in the dates.
3 Spread the mixture in the prepared tin, level the top and sprinkle with the banana chips. Bake in the centre of the oven for 1 hour or until firm to the touch and a skewer inserted in the centre comes out clean. Allow the loaf to cool in the tin for 10 minutes, then turn it out on to a wire rack, peel off the lining paper and leave to cool completely.

SUGAR-FREE CHERRY, DATE AND ALMOND LOAF

Time to make: 30 to 40 minutes
Time to bake: 70 to 80 minutes
Makes a 1 kg (2 lb) loaf that cuts into 8 to 10 slices

125 g (4 oz) ready-to-eat dried apricots
125 g (4 oz) ready-to-eat dried pitted prunes
125 g (4 oz) natural-coloured glacé cherries
125 g (4 oz) ready-to-eat dried dates
185 g (6 oz) Muscatel raisins
155 ml (5 fl oz) orange juice
60 ml (2 fl oz) brandy
2 tablespoons apricot fruit spread with no added sugar
90 g (3 oz) plain wholemeal flour
90 g (3 oz) self-raising flour
½ teaspoon mixed spice
½ teaspoon ground cinnamon
3 eggs, size 4
155 g (5 oz) butter, softened
60 g (2 oz) flaked almonds

Topping

30 g (1 oz) flaked almonds
125 g (4 oz) glacé cherries

Storing and Freezing
Store for up to 2 weeks in a cake tin.
Freeze for up to 2 months in a plastic bag or in an airtight container. Defrost for 8 hours at room temperature.

The inspiration for this cake came from a cafe at one of the British Rail stations. You may not believe this, but I promise you it is true. I was waiting for a train one day and I decided to have a cup of coffee and a slice of cake. The cake was similar to this and so delicious that I decided to re-create the recipe as soon as I got home. I particularly like the result of my experiments as it contains no processed sugar, instead being sweetened by the fruit plumped up in orange juice and brandy. It also contains all my favourite fruits, such as apricots, prunes and dates, so I think it is nice enough to serve as an alternative Christmas cake.

1 Halve the apricots and prunes, then place them into a saucepan over a medium heat with the cherries, dates, raisins, orange juice, brandy and fruit spread. Bring to the boil, then turn off the heat and leave the mixture to cool, stirring occasionally so it cools faster.
2 Meanwhile, set the oven to 150C, 300F, Gas 2. Grease a 1 kg (2 lb) loaf tin and line the base and sides with greaseproof paper, see page 11.
3 Place the flours, mixed spice, cinnamon, eggs, butter and flaked almonds into a large bowl and stir together until well blended. Stir in the cooled fruits.
4 Spread the mixture in the prepared tin (the mixture should fill the tin), level the top and sprinkle with the extra flaked almonds and cherries for the topping. Bake in the centre of the oven for 70 to 80 minutes or until firm to the touch. Allow the loaf to cool completely in the tin on a wire rack, then turn it out and peel off the lining paper.

Opposite: Sugar-free Cherry, Date and Almond Loaf (back) with Rosemary and Lemon Loaf, see page 92

ROSEMARY AND LEMON LOAF

Time to make: 25 minutes
Time to bake: 60 to 70 minutes
Makes a 1 kg (2 lb) loaf that cuts into 10 slices

1 unwaxed lemon
4 branches of fresh rosemary, each about 10 cm (4 in) long
185 g (6 oz) sunflower margarine
185 g (6 oz) caster sugar
3 eggs, size 3
250 g (8 oz) self-raising flour
2 tablespoons milk

Decoration (optional)
2 unwaxed lemons
4 small sprigs fresh rosemary
1 tablespoon icing sugar

Storing and Freezing
Store for up to 1 week in a cake tin. Freeze for up to 1 month in a plastic bag or an airtight container. Defrost for 5 to 6 hours at room temperature.

Photographed on page 91

Having just planted my herb garden, I dreamt of this recipe so I simply had to make it the next day. It is wonderfully perfumed and fresh tasting, but not everyone will guess the surprise ingredient! If you do want to decorate the top, I suggest you caramelise lemon slices for the topping because I like the slightly sweeter taste, but you can leave them raw instead if you prefer a burst of fresh lemon flavour.

1 Set the oven to 160C, 325F, Gas 3. Grease a 1 kg (2 lb) loaf tin and line the base and sides with greaseproof paper, see page 11. Finely grate the lemon rind into a large mixing bowl. Use scissors to finely snip the rosemary needles into the bowl.
2 Add the margarine, sugar, eggs, flour and milk and beat together for 2 to 3 minutes with a wooden spoon until well blended and smooth.
3 Spread the mixture in the prepared tin and level the top. Bake in the centre of the oven for 60 to 70 minutes until firm to the touch and a skewer inserted into the centre comes out clean. Allow the cake to cool in the tin for 10 minutes, then turn it out on to a wire rack, peel off the lining paper and leave to cool completely.
4 You can serve the cake plain or decorate the top. To decorate, thinly slice the lemons and place into a small frying pan over a medium heat with the icing sugar and cook until they are just lightly brown and caramelised. Arrange on top of the cake with the rosemary sprigs.

Cook's Tip
Another way to decorate the top is to put some lemon slices in the base of the greased and lined tin before you add the cake mixture, then glaze them with a little melted honey after you turn out the loaf.

CRUSHED ORANGE AND RAISIN LOAF

Time to make: 15 minutes
Time to bake: 50 to 60 minutes
Makes a 1 kg (2 lb) loaf that cuts into 12 slices

1 unwaxed orange
125 g (4 oz) soft margarine
125 g (4 oz) light muscovado sugar
2 eggs, size 3, at room temperature
185 g (6 oz) self-raising wholemeal flour
1 teaspoon ground cinnamon
3 tablespoons natural yogurt
90 g (3 oz) raisins

Icing
60 g (2 oz) icing sugar

Storing and Freezing
Store for up to 2 weeks in a cake tin. Freeze in a plastic bag or airtight container for up to 3 months. Defrost for 5 to 6 hours at room temperature.

This is a delicious family cake that is very quickly made by whizzing up the flesh of an orange in the food processor and then stirring in the remaining ingredients. It has a slightly chewy texture and takes only minutes to make.

1 Set oven to 180C, 350F, Gas 4. Grease and line a 1 kg (2 lb) loaf tin with greaseproof paper, see page 11. Grease the paper well.
2 Wash the orange, then cut it in half, squeeze the juice and reserve. Chop the rind and flesh roughly, then place into a food processor and blend to a rough paste.
3 Place the orange paste into a large bowl with the margarine, sugar, eggs, flour, cinnamon and yogurt. Mix together well, then beat for 2 to 3 minutes until light and fluffy. Stir in the raisins.
4 Spread the mixture in the prepared tin and level the top. Bake in the centre of the oven for 50 to 60 minutes until firm to the touch and a skewer comes out clean. Turn out of tin, peel off the lining paper and allow to cool completely on a wire rack.
5 To make the icing, mix the icing sugar with 1 tablespoon of the reserved orange juice and drizzle over the top of the cake.

SOUR CHERRY AND CRANBERRY LOAF

Time to make: 20 minutes
Time to bake: 1 hour
Makes a 1 kg (2 lb) loaf cake that cuts into 8 to 10 slices

1 unwaxed orange
185 g (6 oz) butter, at room temperature
185 g (6 oz) caster sugar
2 eggs, size 3, lightly beaten and at room temperature
250 g (8 oz) plain flour
½ teaspoon salt
1 teaspoon baking powder
60 g (2 oz) dried cranberries
60 g (2 oz) dried sour cherries

Topping

4 tablespoons icing sugar
30 g (1 oz) dried cranberries
30 g (1 oz) dried sour cherries

Storing and Freezing
Store for up to 2 weeks in a cake tin.
Freeze without the topping for up to 1 month in a plastic bag or an airtight container. Defrost for 4 to 5 hours at room temperature, then top or simply dust with icing sugar.

This is a new and, I think, nicer version of a traditional plain cherry cake. I've simply used dried sour cherries and dried cranberries with grated orange rind for extra flavour. You can buy dried cranberries and sour cherries in supermarkets and health food shops. They are delicious to nibble and packed full of vitamin C.

1 Set the oven to 180C, 350F, Gas 4. Grease a 1 kg (2 lb) loaf tin and line the base and sides with greaseproof paper, see page 11. Grate the orange rind and squeeze the juice and set both aside separately.
2 Put the butter and sugar into a large bowl and cream together until light and fluffy. Gradually beat in the eggs, adding a little flour if the mixture begins to curdle.
3 Sift over the remaining flour, salt and baking powder together and fold into the creamed mixture, along with the orange rind, cranberries and cherries and 1 to 2 tablespoon orange juice to give a soft dropping consistency; reserve 1 tablespoonful orange juice for the icing.
4 Spread the mixture in the prepared tin and level the top. Bake in the centre of the oven for about 1 hour until firm to the touch. Allow the cake to cool for 10 minutes in the tin, then turn it out on to a wire rack, peel off the lining paper and leave to cool completely.
5 To make topping, sift the icing sugar into a bowl, then stir in about 1 tablespoon orange juice to give the consistency of single cream. Drizzle over the top of the cake, then sprinkle with the additional dried cranberries and sour cherries.

Sour Cherry and Cranberry Loaf

INDEX